114822

How to Start Your Own School

HOW TO START
YOUR OWN SCHOOL

*A Guide for the Radical Right, the
Radical Left, and Everybody In-Between
Who's Fed Up with Public Education*

by ROBERT LOVE

The Macmillan Company · New York, New York

Collier-Macmillan Publishers, London

The Macmillan Company
866 Third Avenue, New York, N.Y. 10022
Collier-Macmillan Canada Ltd., Toronto, Ontario

Library of Congress Catalog Card Number: 72-90275

FIRST PRINTING 1973

Printed in the United States of America

Acknowledgments

WICHITA COLLEGIATE SCHOOL has been a learning experience for all of us. When we started the school, we had no idea of the problems we would encounter. Our only thought was for a better education for our children and we didn't think of other consequences. As a matter of fact, had we known the demands of this undertaking we might not have started. But the rewards have been far greater than we expected and, knowing that, we would do it again tomorrow without hesitation.

Since my children have graduated from Collegiate, I felt it necessary to chronicle these experiences for them and at the same time I'm happy to make the experiences available for others. I can do this now—my children have graduated and the school enrollment is overflowing. On both counts, the school can be considered a success. I would like to see more schools succeed by doing what Collegiate did. By this, I do not mean patterning themselves after Collegiate, but cultivating the desire that Collegiate parents have to participate in the education of their children.

There are some differences in schooling and other undertakings, but these differences are only in terms of the problems encountered, not in the basic goal or endeavor. I'm highly indebted to Terry Catchpole, who did much to organize and write so that this story could be told. The two of us were guided by Terry's wife, Catherine, who attended all of our sessions, typed the notes, and typed the original manuscript. This book represents my own experiences and ideas, but, in all honesty, Terry Catchpole contributed some insights and observations that were most welcome. From his vantage point, he was more objective where Collegiate was concerned.

Gratitude for the push to take the time to do this must go to George Pearson of the Center for Independent Education. George has spent many hours in editing, revising, and talking about the book.

Finally, this leaves the most important group, and that is my family. My wife, Lillian, has to be the beginning. She made the first commitment to burn the bridges; after the bridges were burned, I naturally concurred. So, to her must go the credit for making the crucial decision, which is the difference between standing still and doing something. Naturally, our three children, Randy, Robert, and Rebecca, were the reasons for this whole episode. They carried out their roles as students in such a manner that we never questioned our support of them. As far as Mrs. Love and I are concerned, our children made the commitment to independent education and Collegiate School a real joy.

As mentioned in this book, the philosophical position for Collegiate came out of the desire for the best possible opportunities for our children. We didn't know all of the reasons in the early days, but it didn't take much to discover them once we began our effort to provide a better educational opportunity.

vi

Contents

1

What Is This Book?

*

THIS *is not* A BOOK for people who are looking for a detailed critique of public education. There has certainly been enough criticism of public schools written in the past few years to satisfy even the most outraged parent. Besides, if you have a child in public school, you can probably write your own critique.

This book *is* for people who are looking for an alternative to public education. It is written for parents—especially parents disturbed over the present quality of public schooling and frustrated by their inability to do anything about the situation.

You will not find any magic "answers" here. What you will find is the story of a group of parents in Wichita, Kansas, who were also fed up with the education available locally and started their own school, independent of church and state. Since 1960, this independent school—Wichita Collegiate—has proven that parents, students, and teachers, working in full cooperation toward mutual goals, can provide a better education than that which is available elsewhere.

I was in on this venture from its beginning twelve years ago and have often been asked to describe just how Collegiate School was created and developed, and the reasons why we parents undertook the project. This book is an effort to make the information more widely available to those concerned about the present state of education.

My purpose in writing goes further, however, than merely wanting to tell about a school somewhere in the Midwest. Above all, it is my intention to show that Collegiate School need not be an isolated example of independent education. In describing our experience I have tried to provide an outline of how essentially the same thing can be done by other parents, in other towns and cities across the country.

There is no need for parents to continue being frustrated and angered over unsatisfactory education. It is a wasteful, draining exercise in futility. Instead of contending with the existing system, parents must take their lives into their own hands and educate their children on their own terms. I sincerely hope that this book may prompt some parents to do so, for the children's sake.

Finally, if I had my way and book covers were larger, the name of every parent, student, and teacher ever associated with Collegiate School would be listed as a co-author. In lieu of such a monstrous arrangement, I can only say that, while this is written from my personal point of view, the effort itself represented the dedication and commitment of many people.

2

Monopoly vs. Market, or
How the Normal, Average Parent
Can Help Improve Education

THE ONE SURE WAY we can improve education in America is by making the educational system competitive, with parents and students able to do "comparison shopping." The more independent schools there are, the closer we will come to this goal. No monopoly can tolerate true competition for long, and the public school system *is* a monopoly institution. Any concern that can force the public to be customers and competitors to be supporters enjoys a monopolistic position. This is an accurate description of public schools, which received their exclusive, legal privilege through government charter, just as did the original corporate monopolies.

It is important to discuss public education in terms of monopoly power, since this status is at the root of contemporary education problems and represents the situation which an independent school must face in trying to find a solution. For education to be improved, the monopoly must be ended. And anyone who attempts to raise academic quality by offering alternatives to the established system will have to contend with a powerful monopolistic opposition that cares less for quality than it does for survival.

Collegiate School was not conceived as a step toward eliminating public education, but the attitude of our public "competitors" was brought home to us very quickly. We intended to establish the first independent school in Wichita, Kansas, with grades one through twelve, and Collegiate was going to be competing for the best students in the area. We invited parents to compare Collegiate to the local public schools, to shop around for the best "buy."

The reaction of public school officials was one of outright hostility. "The state has the *right* to educate children," said some, echoing the modern American version of the old concept of the "divine right of kings." "Most parents don't know what's best for their children," said others, "and trained, professional administrators *do* know."

The animosity was understandable within the laws of nature. These people were fighting to protect their livelihood. They were guarding an ideal they had believed in and lived by for many years, as well as defending their source of income. It was a good close-up view of monopoly in action.

Soon we began to understand the connection between this action and our original complaints with public education. All monopolies are detrimental in their effect on the people who must deal with them, pay their inevitably rising prices, and make do with their shoddy products or services. Those monopolies sanctioned by the government, however, are the most dangerous because they have immediate access to the threat of violence, through enforcement powers behind the façade of law.

4

The public school system is a perfect example. The government wants people to think of the system as "free public schooling." We all know the schools are not "free" to the nation's taxpayers. They are not "free" to the child who has to sit in a classroom seven hours a day. Nor are students or parents "free" to decide whether or not to attend.

The idea of providing universal education through use of public funds rests on the premise that many parents who want education for their children cannot afford proper schooling. As soon as public education got underway a century ago, however, the state found that many of the same children whose parents supposedly could not afford schooling really did not want to attend school, even if it was "free."

Such actions could not be tolerated. The thought of thousands of youngsters ignoring the benefits of the "free" school system was an anathema. It was a threat to the privileged institutions and their supporters, who proclaimed that the "entire community" would be "robbed" of its "right to an education" by this "handful of dissident malcontents." When the government cannot persuade people to participate voluntarily in one of its programs, it compels them to do so.

Today any child who does not want to go to school or any parents who do not want their children to attend are subject to coercion by the state and to fines and imprisonment if they continue to resist. It is all perfectly legal.

The law requires every child between certain ages to attend school. Thus education becomes a "free" good with forced consumption—hardly a situation conducive to true learning.

5

The real test for any monopoly, public or private, is to judge what it accomplishes over a period of years during which virtually all competition has been eliminated. With the many government monopolies, this is not a difficult judgment to make. War and taxation are the only monopoly activities governments perform well, thanks to long experience, great enthusiasm, and total absence of private competition.

Any monopoly institution, public or private, is destined to grow insensitive to the needs of the people. As there is no need to worry about patronage, the monopoly need not be accountable to its patrons. This is true whether the institution is the IRS or AT&T, or whether the service is medicine dispensed by the AMA monopoly or education dispensed by the public school monopoly.

In a free market, on the other hand, an institution must serve its customers sensitively and well in order to survive. It is held to account by its patrons and must satisfy their demands or go bankrupt. Such open competition in education would improve academic quality, since those holding ultimate economic authority—the parents—would be the persons with the greatest interest in a child's education.

When Collegiate School started in the late 1950s, I did not conceive of education as an economic good, subject to the laws of the marketplace. At that time I was concerned only with giving my children a better education.

My view of education as an extremely personal producer-consumer relationship developed gradually, as I realized that a successful educational enterprise is one that directs its every effort toward helping the individual student to achieve his maximum potential. Institutions operating in open, free competition with others having

6

similar motivation will be stimulated to provide this service.

Competition provides the stimulation. I have found that, where there is competition in a field of endeavor, quality improves and prices decline (unless there is uncontrollable inflation). This contrasts with the monopoly situation, where quality deteriorates as prices increase. For evidence, I again offer the government monopolies, whose services to the people have grown increasingly inadequate as costs to the taxpayers have gone up steadily.

Public schools have little meaningful competition and, in the best monopolist tradition, their supporters want even less. Traditional private and parochial schools either eagerly emulate public institutions or are coerced by the state into doing so through acceptance of government accreditation and certification regulations.

There is a vacuum of alternatives which can best be filled by schools with no ties to church or state. Independent schools can offer the state genuine competition, provide the public with viable educational choices, and change the total education picture in the country for the better.

Collegiate School is now attempting to fill the vacuum and meet these standards. There is still no free, competitive education market in Wichita, or any place else in the country. For ourselves, no one connected with Collegiate wants the school to have the local independent school monopoly, any more than we want to live with a government school monopoly. More competition is the ideal way to prevent both.

Nationally, I believe the situation is beginning to change. Each year more parents are becoming disillusioned with their present choices of education and are looking for a better way for their children to learn. This means that the need and the market for working alternatives are also growing. The next step is for parents and teachers to declare their independence and to create these alternatives.

3

A History of Collegiate School, or
How We Got into the
Independent Education Business

Next, LET ME TELL YOU the brief history
of one alternative to public education, the story
of how a couple of otherwise normal people came to help
start an independent school. Then I'll tell you how it was
done.

In the winter of 1957-58 my wife and I were living in
an upper-middle-class neighborhood in Wichita, generally
enjoying life among our family and friends. Our three
children were attending a public elementary school two
blocks away, along with two hundred or so other upper-
middle-class youngsters.

The school was, unfortunately, a typical example of
what passes for education in this age. Our children weren't
learning anything and they were growing to dislike education because this school was wasting their time. We
quickly came to share their attitude.

Our oldest son was described by his teacher as the "best
reader" in the fourth grade. I recalled that someone had
once told me that a fourth-grade student should be able

to read the front page of the daily newspaper without any difficulty, so I decided to give Randy this test. He could read very little of it.

Now, this boy might have been a whiz at handling whatever readers they were using in that fourth-grade class. When it came to getting along in the real world, he might as well have been illiterate. And this was supposedly one of the better public schools in the city—wealthy neighborhood, bright kids, go-getter teachers, all that. As far as we were concerned, it wasn't doing the job.

We felt the school was failing our children in many ways. For example, the fourth grade had a program in which the students could go to the city's public library and spend some time reading if they wanted to. It was described as a "voluntary" program.

One day that winter the teacher asked who was going to the library, and Randy said he'd rather not. He didn't have anything against the library, the program, the teachers, or the other kids—he had already been to the library several times on his own and wanted to stay at school and do something else that particular day. Unfortunately for him, he was the only student who felt this way.

The teacher's response was to hold a kangaroo court to make an example of bad little boys who exercise their independence and "spoil things" for the others. Randy hadn't learned yet that, to public school bureaucrats, any display of independence—even in a "voluntary" situation —is worse than a morning without a new memo. He came home after lunch that day, crying in bewilderment, and refused to go back for classes that afternoon.

The truth was that neither of our boys—the other, Bobby, was then a third-grader—*ever* wanted to return to school after lunch. You might ask: What kid ever does *want* to go to school? And my response would be, probably very few—in poor schools. However, if learning is presented as a natural, vital part of a child's life and made to be the exciting adventure it really is, you can't keep the kids away. We didn't know then whether or not this sort of school existed, but we did know that we wanted such an education for our children.

My wife and I decided right after Randy's classroom "trial" that we were about to become public school dropouts. The incident was one among many, and it was the last. We had only one crack at helping to educate our children and we were so determined to have them get a good grounding in the fundamentals—reading, writing, math—that my wife was prepared to take them anywhere in the country, while I stayed in Wichita. Fortunately for our domestic happiness, we didn't have to go this far.

There was a woman in Wichita at that time who had recently started a school for gifted children. She was looking for potential geniuses to nurture, much the same way a track coach watches for future Olympic stars. She had hired some exceptional teachers, made a down payment on an old house, and set up shop.

We enrolled our three children (daughter Becky was in the second grade) in the fall of 1959. After the first day of classes they all came home saying they were never going back there with all those "screwballs."

Right about now you could be thinking that our kids were just a little bit fussy over where they went to school. We were startled by their attitude too and thought we had better investigate. We didn't find any "screwballs," exactly, but we did discover that classes were held in one big room, that this made for a lot of noise and confusion, and that some of the teachers were no better than those we had left behind us (we thought).

But it was not the school's educational methods which we came to object to the most. I believe that there is a great value in unstructured learning and think that a child can learn in almost any situation as long as he is stimulated by a good instructor. In fact, our children did return to school after that first day and did come to enjoy the learning process much more than they had previously.

What we *did* disapprove of was the method of financing the school's operation—or, more properly, *not* financing it. We learned, for example, that some parents were not required to pay tuition or to do work for the school as compensation. Also, no budget had been prepared, based upon what the school might reasonably expect as income. The final straw was the idea that any deficits in the operating costs should be made up by a handful of the parents, those thought to be most able to afford it.

Since we were placed in this latter category, this didn't set too well around our breakfast table. I have been running a business for over twenty-five years and have met and talked with a lot of other businessmen. I have never yet heard of a successful enterprise where one set of customers was asked to pay more for the same product than another set of customers in order to make up the company's deficits.

Naturally, I had to say something.

We planned to register a complaint, but our "break" was otherwise purely spontaneous. At a routine parents' meeting I pointed out that the school was heading for a deficit of something like $50,000 that could not be paid.

Later I was to discover that deficits are sometimes unavoidable in education and I would learn to tolerate an even larger one. But not then.

In the process of discussing the costs and other economics of education at that meeting, it became obvious to those of us who were expected to make up the operational deficits that we would also have to assume responsibility for holding down the overhead or risk seeing it run wild. We would, in other words, have to take over effective administration of the school.

There was no resistance to this conclusion among the ten to fifteen parents who were footing most of the bills. Subsequently, other parents joined us. All of us "dissidents" finally agreed that, while this particular school offered a better education than the public schools, there was still room in the city for a superior school based on the classical education tradition and operated on a sound economic basis.

We were determined to open an independent school operation of our own by January 1, 1960, and we did. Two of us sat down with the school's founder and explained our decision. We asked that she take with her those students she wanted who were willing to go. She left with about twenty pupils and has continued to run her own school.

The rest of us decided to stay in the building the school had been occupying and we had been paying for. There were four teachers to handle twenty-eight students in grades one through six, and we hired a retired public school principal to come in a couple of days a week to take care of administrative details.

The school took off from there. Later that spring we

gave all the students the comparable public school exams for each grade and found they had gone significantly above average. This was partly due to the kids' enthusiasm over their new school. They thought of themselves as "pioneers" and were helping each other to learn, were seeing who could come up with the best name for the school, and were actually doing homework *on their own.*

This spirit also infected the parents. One Saturday a group of fathers decided it was about time someone painted the one-story school building. The other parents heard about our noble "sacrifice" of a cherished weekend day and just about all of them showed up to help.

There was little question that we would keep going the next fall. We hired a headmaster, the twenty-seven-year-old assistant to the president of a Missouri private school. We drew up a $40,000 first-year budget and divided this total equally among the parents. (However, those who really wanted to participate and could not pay their full share received scholarship aid in return for work done at the school.) And the students decided to name their alma mater the Wichita Independent Day School, as that was precisely where, what, and when it was. As I said, our students were *smart.*

That was twelve years ago. The school's name has since been changed to Wichita Collegiate; a preschool, kindergarten, and grades seven through twelve have been added; and enrollment has expanded to approximately four hundred students. In 1963 we built a new schoolhouse (a comfortable one-story brick-and-wood affair that blends in perfectly with the surrounding Kansas prairie) and in 1965 we constructed another just like it to house the high school.

The high point in the school's history so far came when Collegiate graduated its first senior class in 1967. There is, of course, a purely selfish reason for my saying this: Our oldest son, "Randy the Reader," was a member of this class. (Since Randy was in the highest grade—the sixth— when the school first started, this was my incentive for scrambling to add a new grade each year until the school had all twelve; we were not about to send our son somewhere else to finish his education.) There were twelve students in this graduating class and every one of them was succesful in college.

In all, Wichita Collegiate School graduated fifty students between 1967 and 1970. Forty-eight of these were still in college as of spring, 1971, attending schools such as Goucher, Baylor, Oxford, Princeton, Sewanee, and our local colleges and universities. Fifteen of these graduates were semifinalists in the National Merit Scholarship competition and three of them were finalists. Half of the graduates (twenty-four) made their school's dean's list at one time or another. On college entrance exam scores, Collegiate students average almost ninety points higher than the national average: 573 to 485.

That is a brief history of Wichita Collegiate School, how it got started, where it has gone, and what it has accomplished in purely statistical terms. It has never received one cent of public tax money, nor has it relied on special fund-raising campaigns or charity contributions to bail it out of a hole. The school has been run on a businesslike basis, geared to turning out an exceptional product. Along the way my wife and I lost friends and offended relatives. We also formed many new friendships and received as much of an education as any of the students.

Philosophy, or Why We Are Here

I⊤ MAY SEEM presumptuous for something as ordinary as an elementary and secondary school to have a "philosophy." Philosophies, we have been told, are something for stuffy intellectuals, pedants who have no connection with the real world.

I would contend, instead, that many modern institutions fail the public precisely because they do *not* operate from a solid philosophical base. The administrators do not uphold any consistent, logical set of principles, either for their own lives or for the lives of their institutions. They prefer to "keep their options open," to be able to move in any direction at any given moment.

In more realistic terms, however, these administrators are implying that they are afraid to commit themselves or their institutions to any principle or philosophy that may some day prove unpopular with their boss, their customers, the general public—*anyone*. As a result, our institutions today wander from one position to another. They try to please as many people as possible, while in fact they satisfy fewer people every day.

Nowhere is this phenomenon more evident than in our education system. Every year we see a new curriculum "experiment," a new academic "design," a "restructured" classroom idea, a different "educational theme."

There is nothing at all wrong with experiment and innovation—if they grow logically out of a general operating philosophy. The experiments and innovations found in modern education grow out of nothing more than sheer desperation. And I believe the public senses just how desperate school administrators are.

When Collegiate School first began I don't think that any of us saw the school as being much more than a place where our children could learn something. The philosophy that I discuss here developed around the type of education we wanted Collegiate to offer. Above all, the philosophical development has not been *in spite of* the students and their needs, but *because of* what the school was doing for the children.

Declaration of Independence

The operating philosophy at Collegiate School can be described as the belief that the only way to run a school is to run it independently of everyone but students, parents, and teachers. Period.

That means no bumbling bureaucracies of meddling boards of education. Collegiate's "bureaucracy" consists of the headmaster and his secretary, and even then the headmaster helps earn his pay by teaching. As for the Board of Trustees, it learned not to interfere in the day-to-day operations of the school.

Collegiate's teachers have complete authority over their classrooms and are free to teach however they want. Parents or students who have a complaint talk it over with the teacher most directly involved. Unlike the public schools, Collegiate holds no coercive hand over the parents or students who attend. There are no laws compelling attendance at Collegiate. Both parents and students are there because they want to be.

In order to keep the parent and student "customers," the school must produce a high-quality educational product at a price they will pay. The best way to accomplish these inseparable goals is to have both an independent structure, and independence within the structure itself.

Collegiate's independent philosophy extends all the way down the line. It affects the way parents, students, and teachers live, in and out of school. Independence presumes individual responsibility, and responsibility presumes commitment and involvement. Everyone connected with Collegiate School is committed to its success and involved in seeing that success is achieved.

It has been a great thing to see that commitment works, that responsibility works, that independence works. I can only hope that someday more parents may have this experience.

Collegiate was independent of both church and state from the beginning for very practical reasons. All of us had already rejected state-run schools as being a restrictive, inefficient way to educate children. To be consistent, we decided against any association with the state in our new education venture. This meant no special legislative favors, no participation in government loan or grant programs, no state accreditation, and no requirement that we hire only certified teachers.

The one tie with the state that Collegiate was unable

to avoid involved health regulations, and the only time the school sees a government official is when the health inspector comes around to make sure it has enough toilets and drinking fountains.

Yes, we heard the familiar plaint: "Why don't you stay in the public schools, work within 'the system' to make it better?" And our response was: Because disgruntled parents can attend board meetings, write letters, visit teachers, petition administration officials, and the like until they are blue in the face, and what is the result? They may be ignored, they may be ridiculed as "troublemakers," or they may, finally, someday, make some small change—after their children have gone through several grades and the objectionable policy has already had its ill effects.

This attitude among parents, that they should somehow stick it out "within the system," is too common to pass over quickly. Put bluntly, there is *no way* a citizen or group of citizens can penetrate an entrenched bureaucracy and involve themselves without compromise in the operation at hand—exercising the degree of influence and control over their own child that is rightly theirs—short of overthrowing and eliminating that bureaucracy.

The survival instincts of bureaucrats dictate that they do everything possible to frustrate, thwart, and defeat any faction trying to reduce their power or slow their growth. Even the President of the United States, with all his Constitutional power, cannot fully control the bureaucracy which is theoretically subordinate to him. Why do we go on deluding ourselves that we, with far less power, can do any better?

We have seen in recent years that a majority of United States taxpayers cannot influence the activities of the military bureaucracy that their tax dollars support. The national centralist education bureaucracy is not one bit different. And so, we find the military bureaucracy destroying young lives in Vietnam and the education bureaucracy destroying young minds in our schools. The comparison may be ungentle, but I think it is sound.

Parents have virtually no control over what happens to their children in the public schools they are forced to pay for. When parents become convinced a teacher is inadequate, they are powerless to act on their conclusion. When someone comes along who would make a first-class teacher, but didn't take the ridiculous college courses necessary for a certificate, the parents are out of luck.

Parents don't hire or fire teachers, and once tenure is established firing is virtually impossible. Parents have no say in setting up their child's curriculum, or in determining what approach the child will take to learn his subjects. The situation is analogous to a business which gives its customers no choice in selecting a product which, by law, they must purchase.

The children caught in the middle here are the progeny to which most parents devote a good part of their lives. Yet, in public schools a crucial element in the individual's development—his education, his ability to think and to reason—is forfeited to authoritarian strangers with no direct vested interest in what the child is to become.

I would never for a moment suggest that the people who have sent children to Collegiate School were exceptional parents, or loved their children any more than the next parent. The one difference was that we were determined not to turn the rearing of our children over to anyone else —church, state, television, or the street. *We,* as parents, had the greatest vested interest in our children, and we wanted to raise them and educate them ourselves.

Independence and Responsibility

It was all well and good to talk about freedom and independence and say, Yes, we are going to have a school where the parents, teachers, and students run things. The next lesson we learned was that if these ideas were ever going to amount to anything, we had to get deeply involved ourselves.

When I say "involved" I mean more than attending a school meeting now and then and considering parental duty done. I mean accepting the full responsibility for the child's education, realizing that we, the parents, play a more important part in the child's learning process than all the teachers in the world, and then doing something about it.

I came to understand this principle partially through my business experience. As my company was relatively small, I knew about the relationship between decisions and results. Cause and effect were never far apart. I had a strong desire to see the schooling of my children in the same light, and to do so I used the same approach: to obtain the desired effect, my wife and I had to be in on the cause.

To influence the cause, or decision end, we invested all the time, energy, and money that we could. We didn't necessarily have more of these ingredients to spare than anyone else, but we were willing to invest what we did have. I have never once been dissatisfied with the result or the effect.

There were and still are many ways parents could get involved at Collegiate School. A parent-teacher organization is not one of them. There has never been anything resembling a PTA at Collegiate because none of us wanted to go to meetings, plan agendas, or otherwise play political games to see who gets to run the school. The proper place for us, we felt, was at home, helping our children to learn.

This meant establishing a home atmosphere conducive to learning. Parents are just not accustomed to accepting this responsibility. By contrast, attending PTA meetings is an easy way out.

In the early days of Collegiate we learned quickly that part of the responsibility of independence was the parents' creation of this home environment where learning received the maximum emphasis. Since that time, parents applying at the school have been advised to provide this atmosphere if they expect to get the most out of Collegiate for their children. The headmaster explains that the school demands a top-notch effort by all students all of the time, and if such an effort is not forthcoming the teachers do not take the situation up with the student—they go to the parents.

According to Collegiate's philosophy, it is not enough for a child to be told to "go do your homework" when the parent takes no further interest in what the child is studying. It is also wrong, I feel, for a parent to tell a child to read his textbooks while the parents watch television or have a party and do nothing to help the child concentrate on his studies.

Students cannot learn to the full extent of their capabilities in a home where the parents are unavailable or unwilling to help with lessons, answer questions, and talk over ideas. Such a home life will result in a below-par academic performance and unless the child is an exceptional student, he will fall behind.

The blame in these cases lies entirely with the parents. Unfortunately, it is the child who must bear the scar of a poor education.

To help avoid the situation, Collegiate parents are confronted directly with the question: Whose child is this and who is responsible? No one expects parents to give up all their leisure activities or completely forgo social engagements (although I do know some Collegiate parents have virtually stopped going out on school nights when their children are studying). Parents are expected to know what is going on in the classroom—what their children are learning, from whom, how, and how well.

The school believes that direct involvement in the child's learning process is the best way for parents to know the school, as well as what it is doing with and to their children. Familiarity does not breed contempt. Full exposure brings cooperation. Taking a personal interest makes the parents subjective, and their interest, participation, and sense of responsibility in their children's education increase the more subjective they become.

It is through direct, subjective involvement that Collegiate School's independent philosophy has been brought into the home. The parents understand that they must create a home atmosphere which stresses learning and in many cases this has meant a complete change in life-style. The parents read more widely and pay more attention to what their children are thinking and studying, and the family discusses ideas on a higher level than it had before. Many, many parents have told me that Collegiate is a total way of life for them, influencing the entire family. I know this was the case in our family.

The parents' actions and involvement affect the independence of both students and teachers. The students are known by the work they do in the classroom. The teachers are known by the students they produce. The rich home environment, conducive to learning, is the root of Collegiate's success—its scholastic success and the success of its independent philosophy. Responsibility works.

A word here about student responsibilities. The children who attend Collegiate cannot help but be aware of the commitment their parents have made to their education. They see this (or should see it) every day in their homes. The students realize that this independent school offers them an education that is, at least to their parents' minds, the best that can be obtained.

The parents and teachers are responsible for providing the best education and the best means to an education that they can, and the students understand that they are responsible for absorbing what this education has to offer. If they are to take full advantage of the education available, the students' commitment must match that of their parents. That means learning.

Collegiate students have more independence within the school than they would in most other schools. They are free to learn at their own speed, to the full extent of their intellectual capability. And, although they are perfectly normal children, rarely do these youngsters abuse this freedom. They are self-disciplined, hard-working, and respectful of the freedom of others.

When Collegiate began adding secondary grades to the school the older students got together and formed a student government. They held meetings and kicked around resolutions, spending a couple of hours each week without getting into trouble.

After a short while the "government" withered away. The would-be politicians had found there was nothing to do, no reason for a government of any kind at Collegiate School. They couldn't pass any rules governing the other students because everyone was responsible for himself. Government was a waste of time. The students found they could pass the time better concentrating on learning. That was the way they wanted it.

There have been students who have, for reasons of their own, chosen not to accept the situation at Collegiate once they were enrolled. This is the students' choice and they are free to make it, no questions asked. Collegiate has neither the means nor the desire to keep students who do not wish to be there.

There is another side to the independence-responsibility matter, namely, knowing when *not* to get involved. This is especially important in parent-teacher relationships. The parents—including the trustees who are also parents— had to learn to extend to the teachers the same independence they wanted for themselves and for the school.

The Collegiate teachers are hired because they have something to offer the children, whether they have a dozen degrees or never graduated from high school. Once employed, the teachers are judged by parents, students, and other teachers according to the students they produce. If an instructor's product is found to be inferior, he or she will be dismissed.

This again is a basic producer-consumer relationship. When the producer turns out an unsatisfactory product, the consumer withdraws his patronage. The producer is paid according to the quality of his work, and his professional reputation depends on the acceptance of that work by his peers and the customers.

The same hands-off rule applies to all members of the Board of Trustees: no interfering with what the teachers are doing in the classroom. Part of the burden of being responsible for your own actions is the willingness to allow the teachers to be responsible for theirs. Another lesson borrowed from my business experience: never separate authority and responsibility.

These attitudes, which look so fine and noble in print, did not develop overnight in any of us. Collegiate parents were and are themselves products of the public schools and have never known any other kind of education. Evolving a sound operating philosophy of independent education takes time, takes making mistakes, takes patience. There are neither teachers' contracts nor tenure at Collegiate. Faculty members can resign whenever they please, and it would be a disservice to the parent and student customers if Collegiate tried to force a teacher to stay. The teachers receive their assignments and are put completely on their own, free to succeed or fail as the head of their own little "business" within the school.

Parents, meanwhile, may determine a teacher's fate, but only if it is the teacher and not they who are responsible for a bad academic performance. Many parents have come to the headmaster complaining about the way some teacher was being "unfair" or "too hard" on their child, when everyone knew that the parents hadn't done a thing to help the child learn. In those cases the teacher stays and the parents usually leave.

The parents cannot tell the teachers what to teach or how to teach, no matter how much time or money they have put into the school. They can take suggestions for curriculum changes to the headmaster and many of these have been adopted by the school. But we have had parents who tried a more forceful approach, including a $250,000 offer to the school with the proviso that there be no homework. The offer was refused.

Neither my wife nor I have ever tried to strike this sort of bargain, but we have had our differences with Collegiate teachers, sometimes major differences. They stayed, so did we.

Two Men, Two Ends: An Aside

Not everyone associated with Collegiate School was in total agreement on the independent philosophy. No one was made to sign a loyalty oath, nor sworn to silence. A parent or trustee having an objection could offer it for discussion at any time. If the result of the discussion was unsatisfactory, the objector was free to go.

So far, we have had one major incident where someone did leave the school. I will describe the episode because I think it underscores the difference between Collegiate's approach and that of conventional education and also demonstrates how committed we were to independent education.

I will call the lead character Mr. Public Education. He had been with Collegiate since its founding and had, in fact, been one of those parents who had taken their children out of the original school to help establish the Independent Day School. By the time the incident in question occurred, Mr. P. E. had been a member of Collegiate's Board of Trustees for several years and his children were attending the school.

A good part of Mr. P. E.'s disagreements with the school was caused by differences between him and me on a practical political level. During the first days of our independent school venture and throughout its development period, I was a member of the National Council of the John Birch Society. I resigned this position in 1968 because of my opposition to our country's policy in Vietnam. I thought the United States should end its interference in the Vietnamese civil war, and the Society thought we should bomb Hanoi. But in 1966 I was still a member of the council.

Mr. P. E. and I did not agree on much of anything in the political sphere, but we both wanted a good education for our children and were able to work together at Collegiate. By the mid-sixties, however, what with anti-Birch propaganda bursting forth across the nation, Mr. P. E. began expressing fears that I was using my position as chairman of the Board of Trustees to transform Collegiate into a "right-wing school."

To prevent any such outside interference in the classroom, Mr. P. E. asked members of the Board of Trustees to sign a resolution he had prepared, saying that the trustees promised to keep hands off the teachers. Maybe he thought that I would not sign the resolution. I was the first to sign and Mr. P. E. was the first to intercede. He went directly to a teacher with suggestions on what to teach and what not to teach.

Mr. P. E. had other objections. He disapproved of the speeches made by Collegiate trustees and the headmaster in which government education was criticized and independent education was encouraged as a preferable alternative. Although Mr. P. E. had helped to found an independent school and had enrolled his children in the

29

school, he still maintained, he said, "a good deal of respect" for public schools.

At one board meeting Mr. P. E. quoted favorably the observation, made by the head of another independent school, that "recognition of the problems faced by public schools and the magnificent way in which they are usually tackled is the precursor to a genuine hospitality toward the aims and methods of public and private education generally. It is sheer nonsense to say that public and private education are incompatible or that they cannot work together. They can and they do."

The majority of those committed to Collegiate School, then and now, disagreed with this statement. Not only did we have our criticisms of public school education, but we had come to favor an independent education market where many different types of schools and educational methods would compete, offering parents a wide range of learning opportunities for their children. Government-run education is the very antithesis of such a goal, and education bureaucrats abhor any competition.

Differences of opinion came to a head. The Board of Trustees was asked to take a vote-of-confidence in the board chairman—me—and the school's headmaster. The vote was taken and all but Mr. P. E. voted to continue on the course already set by the board.

Mr. P. E. remained true to his convictions. He resigned from the board and removed his children from Collegiate. After leaving, Mr. P. E. was elected to the Wichita Board of Education and later was elected president.

His term on the public school board was quite eventful. In the late 1960s the U.S. Department of Health, Education and Welfare charged the Wichita public schools with de facto segregation. While the city's high schools were integrated years ago, the neighborhood elementary schools, given the discriminatory housing pattern and absence of busing, remained segregated as the school district lines constantly changed to please Wichita's approximately 90 percent white population.

Following the HEW citation, hearings were held and the case for neighborhood schools was presented to a federal examiner. The government would not be moved. HEW reaffirmed its charge and withdrew the several million it was annually giving the city. This figure represented a small percentage of the total education budget, but it influenced out of proportion the operation of the entire Wichita public school system.

While Mr. P. E. was still active at Collegiate we had several conversations about our respective theories of education. I had always contended that federal aid means federal control and that this creates an unresponsive operation: the student-consumers don't buy, the faculty-producers don't sell, and the taxpayer-owners don't control. When there is federal control, the government can do just as it pleases and the schools and parents can do little but acquiesce.

Mr. P. E. did not agree. When he left Collegiate and agreed to serve on the public school board he was determined to work "within the system" to show that the community, and not the government, could control the public schools. HEW showed how wrong he was.

Mr. P. E. had followed his convictions and tried his best to "recognize" public school problems and work to improve them. But at the end of his term he chose not to run for reelection and retired from the Board of Education. I believe that I also have remained true to my convictions and I am still active at Collegiate School.

When Is a School like the YMCA?

In the financing of Collegiate School we introduced a notion that is common in business but radical in the field of education: we insisted that income from tuition cover the operating costs. As the school's independent philosophy was applied all the way down the line, Collegiate had to be able to stand on its own feet financially.

Education may not commonly be thought of as a marketable commodity like soybeans or television sets, but it nevertheless is. Constructing facilities and paying teachers requires scarce resources that could be allocated to provide other goods or services. If these resources go to education they are not available elsewhere. In this respect, education is an economic good very similar to soybeans and TVs.

Before education or any goods or service can be adequately delivered, the costs of the expended resources have to be provided by somebody. In the case of Collegiate School it was decided that the "somebody" would be those using its educational facilities and services. No one else.

My first experience in applying these business principles to a noncommercial institution occurred when I became active in the Wichita YMCA, a couple of years before Collegiate started. At that time, in 1957, the YMCA was on the edge of bankruptcy and about to be disbanded. The people in the community who voluntarily supported the "Y" contended that financing it was becoming a burden, that its programs were inadequate, and that it might as well be scrapped.

Members of the YMCA Board of Directors thought this

would be a tragedy for the children of the community, and we looked for a way to save the "Y." We started with a basic philosophy. The "Y's" former philosophy could be expressed as "Don't ask anyone to pay, but give everyone services." We changed this to "Everyone should be asked to pay, but no one will be denied services."

The YMCA's baseball program is a good example of the change we made. The "Y" had been charging each boy $1 for ten weeks of summer baseball. Now, anyone can tell that this was a remarkably low fee considering the equipment, facilities, and personnel time involved. We analyzed the program and found the baseball program actually cost $7.50 per boy for ten weeks.

This meant that there was a $6.50 deficit being underwritten by someone else. Who was it? The money came from the United Fund of Wichita. Many parents who gave to the United Fund with the idea of helping others less fortunate were actually subsidizing their own children in the YMCA baseball program.

We had a meeting of parents whose children were active in the "Y." I asked them if they gave money to the United Fund with the idea of getting it back, in the form of a subsidy, through the YMCA. "Of course not," they said.

So, we raised the baseball program fee to $7.50, its full cost. Our new policy was not to deny services or use of the facilities to anyone, but to ask everyone to pay. We found that a large percentage could pay their own way, with money from contributions covering those who could not afford the full cost of participation.

If people are given a good program and are asked to pay their share of what the program actually costs, they will. Then a number of participants who cannot pay the full amount, or perhaps nothing at all, can be included. All the "Y" asked was that people be responsible for themselves.

With the new $7.50 charge, the YMCA was able to offer its services to more youths than ever before—including those from low-income families who could not pay—and the program improved as increased funds became available for better equipment, umpires, grounds-keeping, etc. Soon other city baseball leagues were flourishing, able to compete with the YMCA in quality and price. Baseball in Wichita was improved as a result of charging what it cost, instead of giving it away.

The new philosophy was applied to the entire YMCA operation, and every year revenues and the number of participants have grown. The percentage of its annual budget which the Wichita YMCA receives from the United Fund dropped from 31 percent in 1957 to 11 percent in 1971. The United Fund people couldn't believe it: All their other member organizations were asking for more.

Collegiate School's approach to education is similar to the new approach of the YMCA. Each year Collegiate's headmaster draws up an expense budget for the school year, and the total is proportioned among the parents wanting their children to attend during that year.

Collegiate is treating education as an economic goods. The charges to customers must at least equal the costs incurred in providing the service. We realize that the basic economic principle of "There ain't no such thing as a free lunch" can be applied to education and baseball programs, as well as to midday meals.

If Collegiate's customers value the school's services, they pay the fee being charged. If too many customers are dissatisfied and not enough income is generated, Collegiate is out of business. That is precisely the way it should be.

In the public school system, everyone—old folks, childless couples, bachelors, everybody—pays through the nose, and no one is held accountable for the income produced. And no amount of yelling "accountability" will result in the basic changes necessary. Public education costs increase steadily (with no appreciable increase in quality), school boards raise taxes, and when local resources dry up —through tax lids or public rejection of bond issues— the schools turn to the federal government. The government can print and distribute all the money it wants through the Federal Reserve, and it's difficult, if not impossible, to hold someone accountable.

Collegiate refuses to accept government money and cannot print its own. Every cent of income has to be carefully budgeted to prevent waste.

I said earlier that Collegiate teachers were left on their own, and this is true insofar as their classroom independence is concerned. It does not mean, however, that they are left unaudited.

It would be ridiculous for Collegiate's Board of Trustees —or the board of trustees of any business—not to audit employee performance and hold people responsible for the monies they use. Over the years we have developed an excellent system for pinpointing Collegiate's costs and for determining how many students it will take to pay the overhead in each class. Everything is then directed at the teacher personally. Each of them is placed in charge of a single economic unit within the school's financial structure.

Should teachers think their budget or their salary is insufficient, they know how to get more the next year: by doing an outstanding job in the classroom, the teacher can raise the quality and reputation of Collegiate's educational service, and this will attract more students and, therefore, greater income from tuition. Once all classrooms are full, then increased salaries must come from reduced costs and/or increased tuitions.

Collegiate had to develop teachers and administrators who not only accepted but believed in the principles of accountability and full-cost tuition. It took these people some time to learn their lessons in the economics of education, and Collegiate had deficits for the first few years.

These deficits were viewed as being nothing more than the tangible symptoms of economic growing pains—the capital investments found in any young enterprise—and they were paid off as the school's service, its quality established, began to sell.

5

Accreditation and Certification, or Just Because You're Better Doesn't Make It Right

IF THE STATE EDUCATORS have their way, the practical application of Collegiate's independent philosophy will come to mean that, within their interpretation of the law, every one of the school's students must be considered a truant. The Kansas truancy statute requires that all children must attend a "school" taught by "competent" instructors. This legislation was enacted years ago when parents were considered to be primarily responsible for the education of their children and concerned enough to satisfy themselves as to the adequacy of the schooling for their children. Now that the educational process has become thoroughly politicized, the government educators are taking the position that, under the truancy statute, a school is a school only if it is accredited by the state, and a teacher is not competent unless certified in accordance with government regulations and standards. Every other public, private, and parochial school in the state except Collegiate has been accredited by the state Board of Education, which means that all faculty members must be certified. Collegiate is accredited only by the Independent School Association of the Southwest, a private organization which grants accreditation to member schools based upon their educational performance.

This resistance to the government educational establishment has not adversely affected either the school or its "truant" students. None of Collegiate's graduates has had any difficulty gaining admission to college. Although no one can predict the outcome if the state ever tries to bring Collegiate into line with the other schools in Kansas, I doubt if those associated with the school will ever voluntarily change its status. We have dealt with education officials enough to know that their accreditation and certification requirements do not guarantee quality education, and we can only hope that the courts will also understand this if they are ever presented with the issue in Kansas.

The usual means by which individual states exercise control over the schools within their boundaries is to require by law that all children between certain ages attend an "accredited" or an "approved" school. A school achieves this status by employing only teachers who have been "certified," meaning that they have taken prescribed "education" courses at a college or university whose education department has itself been "approved" and "accredited" by the government.

I frankly admit that when our education venture began we didn't have much cause to question the accreditation-and-certification game. It seemed a simple matter to follow course and request state accreditation. In the first years Collegiate's faculty was, coincidentally, comprised totally of disgruntled former public school teachers who were all certified.

38

Soon, however, we hired some uncertified teachers and innocently sent their credentials, along with those of our headmaster, to the state Board of Education. The state returned a long list of college courses our teachers would have to take before they could meet the Kansas certification requirements. The headmaster had to meet the same requirements before he could teach a class, and he had formerly administered the teacher-training program at a large state university!

There was a flaw somewhere in the state's argument, and the new headmaster helped put us on the track when he invited some Collegiate trustees to have lunch with the chairman of the Education Department of a nearby state university. During the course of the conversation the headmaster asked the educator why it is that the professors who teach the education courses in a university aren't required to have taken the same courses—and be certified —themselves.

The question was never answered. How could this professional educator explain to a group of neophytes why teachers who teach the elementary and secondary school teachers can't teach in elementary and secondary schools themselves? I'm sure we would not have understood even if he had explained.

What made the luncheon lesson doubly effective was the fact that the president of that same university at that time had been a lecturer at Collegiate School, yet was forbidden by law to teach at a state-accredited school. He was not a certified teacher, and by inviting the president of the university to conduct a class, a school could lose its state accreditation.

It finally dawned on the other trustees and me that

accreditation and certification are a lot of hokum. The state's certification rules require prospective teachers to take a number of teaching methodology courses, which means that they take that many fewer courses in their specialty field. These arbitrary standards are, moreover, absolute minimum standards, requiring courses which demand no great intellectual effort on the part of the aspiring teacher. Certification is unmistakably a threat to academic quality.

When Collegiate's trustees questioned members of the Accrediting Division of the Kansas State Department of Public Instruction concerning the certification possibilities of the headmaster and teachers, they conceded that Collegiate's faculty had better college grade averages and a broader academic background than it required of certified teachers. Yet the same teachers, as well as the headmaster, were not eligible for certification. Collegiate's people *exceeded* the average qualifications of teachers in Kansas, but did not *meet* the state requirements.

A few Collegiate parents remained concerned that lack of accreditation might somehow endanger their children's chances of getting into college when it came time for them to apply. At the urging of these skeptics, the trustees called a meeting and invited a member of the accrediting division to explain accreditation.

The guest educator was describing the standards Collegiate teachers didn't meet and why, when one of the parents, a Harvard graduate, spoke up. "Very well, sir," he said to the visiting official, "if we don't meet these requirements now, tell me, if our children leave Collegiate and go on to Harvard and Vassar and do well, would the state board then consider Collegiate to be a good school?"

The state representative looked his inquisitor right in the eye and replied: "Sir, I have no idea what the standards of Harvard and Vassar may be." That remark convinced every parent in the room. The Board of Trustees voted to table the subject of accreditation and certification, and not one parent objected. It has never been brought up again.

It has since been demonstrated to all of us that colleges and universities pay no attention to whether an applicant has been to an accredited secondary school. When it comes to a student's academic abilities, admissions officers look at the applicant's College Board exam scores and not at where he learned. The only "disadvantage" our students face is their exclusion from a state law guaranteeing graduates of accredited Kansas schools admission to at least one semester at a state-supported university. Collegiate students, however, have been able to make it into these colleges on their own.

The one area in which Collegiate has been handicapped is in athletic competition. The Kansas High School Athletic Association (KSHAA), which controls all interschool sports, tournaments, music festivals, and extracurricular competitive activities in the state, had a provision in its bylaws which said any "accredited" institution could join. When Collegiate applied for KHSAA membership it was given temporary approval because we took the position that we were in the process of being accredited by the Independent School Association of the Southwest (ISAS).

A month later the athletic association voted to reword its bylaws. They now read that "any institution accredited by the state" could join. Collegiate did not fulfill the new requirement, of course, and our application for membership was rejected.

Some parents wanted very much for their children to have the experience of interschool athletics, and Collegiate went ahead and scheduled some football and basketball games with any schools in the area which would play them. The KHSAA responded to this show of disloyalty by saying it would expel any Kansas schools that dared play Collegiate teams. Our trustees immediately threatened the athletic association with a civil rights suit and the issue was dropped. We have since developed a very active athletic program with other schools, the only "restriction" being that Collegiate cannot play in the KHSAA-sanctioned state tournaments—the bureaucracy's "last word" to us.

As our knowledge and understanding of how the bureaucracy regulates education increased over the years, our position regarding Collegiate School was reinforced. We became convinced that no one can judge our school and its teachers as well as the students who attend Collegiate and the parents who send them. The customers would not tolerate poor teachers at Collegiate because they were not about to pay $1000 or more a year in tuition for an incompetent faculty. When the customer has ultimate control over a school and its teachers, no state requirements are needed.

Once the accreditation-certification debate was over, Collegiate could concentrate on hiring competent—not merely certified—teachers. The school looked for college graduates who were trained in their specialty. If the school was seeking an English teacher, it wanted someone who had majored in English. It wanted someone who had taken a lot of English courses in college, not a person who had spent up to 25 percent of his college time taking methodology education courses.

In considering applications for teaching positions, Collegiate's headmaster takes into consideration the applicant's range of college courses, grade average, any writing, the leadership positions held in college or in the community, and the applicant's self-analysis of what he has to offer Collegiate students. The emphasis is on extent and breadth of knowledge.

This approach has resulted in Collegiate's hiring a number of young college graduates with liberal arts background as upper-school teachers. We have found that liberal arts schools are full of people who would like to try teaching, but who do not want to waste their time on the education courses required for certification. Because these people avoid courses lacking intellectual challenge and content, public schools cannot consider them for employment and the nation's children are deprived of some excellent instructors.

The young liberal arts graduates were not even certain they wanted to make a career out of teaching when Collegiate hired them. But even when these faculty members found they did not really like teaching, it was only after they had given Collegiate students two or three years of stimulating learning.

Actually, the school discovered the pedagogical value of liberal arts graduates almost by accident. In the school's second year we received applications from two young fellows just out of eastern colleges (Brown and Boston University) who wanted to try their hand at teaching in the Midwest. The headmaster, believing they had more to offer than an education major, took a gamble and one fellow stayed four years, the other for three years. Both taught the high school students everything they had just learned in college.

Collegiate has also had some rewarding experiences hiring people who decided relatively late in life that they would like to teach. Perhaps the best teacher in the school's brief history was a former Jesuit monk who came to Collegiate when he was thirty-five. Drawing on his background in classical literature, he gave a depth of excellence to our English courses that has endured and he developed Collegiate's excellent humanities program. When his voice failed three years after joining our faculty and he had to stop teaching, it was a great loss to the school.

Another "late-bloomer" was a man who had been a steelworker in Pennsylvania for twenty years before deciding he wanted to teach. He went back to college, received his M.A., and was hired to teach history and economics at Collegiate when he was forty-one. Our French teacher was a Mennonite missionary in the Congo until he was run out by the Lumumba government in 1961 and returned to the safety of Kansas and teaching.

Flexibility in faculty hiring is something that an independent school should exploit to its full advantage. It will benefit the students and the school. Collegiate has hired the best people—not necessarily "teachers"—it could find, paid them very well and got as much out of them as they could give.

Maybe these people didn't know how to handle every classroom "crisis" or how to deliver a professional lecture when they first arrived, but those who were competent learned quickly. Of course, along with the competent, good teachers have come those who were not so good. This only reconfirms what I have learned in business: no one can tell how well a man will perform a job until he starts doing it, and those who usually spot a bad worker first are the customers.

Collegiate's teaching innovations are further evidence of its flexibility. In 1972, for example, the senior students began serving as teacher's aides in any grade or course they chose, in lieu of taking one course. The headmaster would like to use more parents as teacher's aides, tutors, and faculty members. And I am looking forward to the day when former Collegiate students graduate from college, return to Wichita to live and work, and can come to the school to give class lectures.

Any school wishing to be independent and successful must have, and use, this flexibility. No outside authority should dictate the terms of the education a school may offer. This includes the state, with its accreditation and certification requirements.

Parents must resist attempts to regulate the independent school if they truly care about the quality of its education. Educational bureaucracies always think they know better than the parents what is best for the child. It is up to the parents to decide whether this is true. If the parents decide it is not the case and resist, they must be prepared to live with the consequences.

After the first couple of years, Collegiate parents have not spent much time worrying about accreditation and certification. The people associated with the school thought highly enough of their own judgment and their right to control the education of their own children to make further debate over accepting state regulation in any form unnecessary.

45

If providing the type of education we wanted for our children meant the children could legally be classified as "truants," that was the price Collegiate parents had to pay. No one connected with the school has ever lobbied for some political-legislative dispensation that would permit the school to exist as it wanted. The parents have always felt that if the school's independent status is ever challenged by the state, the quality of its educational program will prove to anyone, beyond any doubt, that Collegiate is a good school.

Consumption, or

To Market, To Market

THE MOST FORMIDABLE JOB of education
Collegiate School ever faced was to convince
the parents of Wichita that it was in the best interests of
them and their children to enroll at this independent
school. We were all confident from the outset that there
was a market in Wichita for the type of education Collegiate offered, at the price it charged. Getting the potential
customers to become actual customers required a substantial "education" effort.

The situation we were up against—and still face, for
that matter—is one which any self-respecting businessman
would go out of his way to avoid. Collegiate School was
entering a business field in which all its potential customers
were forced to buy a competitor's product, then throw it
away unused if they decided to purchase Collegiate's service. Every parent we have ever approached has already
paid for one education, and our job has been to persuade
them that they should make another purchase that would
be better for their child.

We faced this situation, moreover, in an area where the

idea of public schooling is revered. Public schools came early to the prairie frontier and were willingly supported by the townspeople. The proper young schoolmarm arriving in town to run the little one-room schoolhouse, after a long, dusty train ride from Philadelphia, is a legendary heroine in America's western culture.

The majority of parents we talk to have been to public school and instinctively feel that what was good enough for them ought to be good enough for their children. Not only individual parents, but industry and the professions tend obediently to accept the standards of public education as their criteria for intellectual achievement. Out here, at least, the public *believes* in public schools and accepts the government's influence over educational standards.

Of course every private school in the country faces, to some degree, the economic and social situation confronting us in Wichita. But the others have advantages never enjoyed by Collegiate. Church-affiliated schools have the appeal of religious training, plus the fact they require little or no tuition. Exclusive, established private schools offer an academic reputation and social status for both parent and student. Private military schools have a disciplinary appeal.

Collegiate School, like any new independent school, had to make it on the quality of its education, of its personnel, and the merits of its operating philosophy. As the first independent school in Kansas, we had to make the argument for alternative education as it never had been made before in our community.

The biggest hurdle we faced in our "educational" effort among the parents was in getting them to accept the idea that a superior education was *worth* paying "extra" for.

This was a far more crucial and difficult accomplishment than getting them actually to write out a check and pay the tuition. There have been cases where very wealthy parents, who could afford to send ten children through Collegiate, refused to believe that their children's education was a worthwhile investment.

The first reaction we would encounter in talking to parents was: "Why should I send my children to Collegiate when I can send them to public school for free?"

"But you are not getting a public education for 'free' and here's what it costs you," we would reply. And we would show them that the amount they would pay in property taxes to support public schools over a forty-year home-ownership period could easily reach a total exceeding the amount needed to send two children to Collegiate for the full twelve years.

These people had not considered education on such simple economic terms. I suspect that when they said, "I don't mind paying my taxes for public education," the underlying thought was, "I don't mind paying my taxes for public education . . . as long as everybody else is forced to pay, too." This is a natural attitude. The parents had not been challenged to examine their attitudes before, and when we confronted them with the question, "If education truly cost $1000 a year, would you still pay it?" Many immediately replied, "Yes, if that's what it costs. I don't want to be subsidized by somebody else."

Don't get the idea that parents are always this easy to convince—not when the matter of paying directly for education comes to most parents only after their children are almost out of high school and ready for college. Even this experience wasn't much help to us in Kansas, where a resident can put his child through four years at a state university for less than it costs to send him to Collegiate for the same period. The parochial schools did not help us to educate the public, either, as the tuition they charged (usually around $200 a year) was considerably less than full-cost.

Even parents who did decide to send their children to Collegiate did not immediately adjust to making direct expenditures for education. For most parents it still takes a year or two before the allocation for education was as much a part of the basic family budget as the cash outlay for food, clothing, and shelter.

An ironclad argument for independent education had to be made before parents reached the point of viewing good education as a fundamental family need. Our argument had to transcend the economics involved. Although *we* were convinced that Collegiate School offered the best education for miles around, this was not so evident to everyone else in town. We had to buttonhole every friend, relative, and associate we could find, and use every method of persuasion short of kidnaping to get their children enrolled.

Finally, after a period of trial-and-error testing of our arguments, we found that the case for independent education could be best presented to prospective parents in these terms: you have only one chance to educate your children, and you can never be certain you are doing the best for them; the most you *can* do is to increase the odds on the child's access to the best educational opportunity that is available. Put in this context, we contended that Collegiate was a better gamble than any other school in our community.

To make this "gamble" seem less like a game of education roulette, we had to develop an outstanding faculty, curriculum, and operating philosophy as rapidly as possible. The people of Wichita had nothing with which to compare us except the public and parochial schools, and because these schools were low-cost or free they were not a helpful comparison.

We also were aware that the community was not disposed toward independent education. Collegiate's trustees, administrators, and teachers—who had all gone through public schools themselves—had no great enthusiasm for this new idea. Whether we liked it or not, our school could not begin by shattering the public school image. We were unproven, unknown, and completely without credibility.

Collegiate had to start from scratch and start slowly. We had to look something like a public school, and perform much better. Then, over a period of years, we could change our style and pull the market in our direction. This approach may not sound very romantic or radical, but it was what we had to do. It represented a realistic appraisal of the market situation we faced. The school simply could not risk offending vast numbers of potential customers and hope to survive.

The first task we faced was separating Collegiate from the reputation private schools had at that time, that of serving as a haven for children with disciplinary and academic problems. In our area private schools were known as a place where rich folks sent their "snotty, spoiled brats." If Collegiate was to demonstrate how an independent school could be financially self-sufficient, free from ties to church or state, and offer a better education than

51

other schools, the label of "academic reformatory" would be a severe hindrance.

The way an institution can avoid a bad reputation is to close the door to those who can create it. Accordingly, Collegiate's trustees decided to admit only students with an I.Q. of at least 100, preferably 110 or over. Parents whose children could not be disciplined or motivated to learn in another school were politely turned away. In later years the school has refused parents wanting their children to come to Collegiate in order to escape the busing plans in public schools. Collegiate has always sought customers who wanted to become involved in the school and the children's learning experience, not political, disciplinary, or academic refugees.

In the early days of Collegiate a number of parents decided against sending their children to the school for reasons that were strictly nonacademic—the political connotations outsiders placed on the school, its lack of social acceptability, its leaders' vocal criticism of public education, etc. We were sorry, at that time, to see people rejecting Collegiate for what we felt to be wrong reasons.

More recently, Collegiate has refused to accept children of parents who wanted to enroll their children for wrong reasons. While no one can ever be sure of a person's true reasons for doing anything, Collegiate had to be as selective as it could and still keep the enrollment up. It was essential that we avoid the problems, headaches, and bad name that a bunch of irresponsible parents could give Collegiate.

(I should say here that on several occasions I have tried to encourage parents of children with an I.Q. in the 60-100 range to start a separate school for these youngsters, and have offered whatever assistance Collegiate could give. However, it appears that the lower a child's I.Q., the less apparent the difference between an independent education and a public education becomes, and the less willing parents are to invest the time and money to start a new school. We have had parents with lower-I.Q. children offer Collegiate sizable contributions if it would waive its standards for their youngsters; but they did not want to make the effort to develop a separate school. I still maintain that an independent education, perhaps integrated with Collegiate's facilities, would be a tremendous help to children in this category, and hope some day to see this proven.)

In "selling" Collegiate to parents concerned with their children's education and the one chance they had in life to ensure the best education, we pointed out that it could offer an academic environment where the odds on quality learning were high. The school provided independence and flexibility within a structure that appeared something like the familiar public schools, but the benefits to the student were far greater.

The teachers were not forced to teach to the lowest intelligence level in a class, as they would be in a school supported by the taxes of every citizen. Also, the individual capabilities in a particular class would have a much smaller range than that found in other schools. Instead of teachers and students trying to work in a class where the I.Q. range might be 50-to-150, at Collegiate the figures were more likely to be 110-to-150. With this concentration, everyone accomplished more.

A school which encourages independence will attract teachers and students who want to take advantage of the freedom. Neither is bound by any sort of strict class regimentation. If a freshman at Collegiate can do the junior English program, he is put in a junior English class. If teachers think a student needs extra help in a subject, they take time during the day to give the child tutorial aid.

Every student at Collegiate—fast, slow, and medium learners—gets "special attention" from his teachers. Students are not all treated the same. As the students' parents are paying directly for a service, the youngsters are treated as individual customers with particular needs. The greatest thing Collegiate can do is to give a child the independence to get the maximum education within the limits of his intellectual capability.

This is the essence of the argument we have made to parents, why we feel that Collegiate represents such an excellent education "gamble." Once this case has been presented successfully, there is still more convincing to be done. This is our second hurdle, having parents pay the tuition once they accept Collegiate's educational benefits. Parents who recognize the potential advantages of Collegiate to their children may still be reluctant to pay twice for the child's schooling. This involves a question of personal values, a matter which no one at Collegiate School could—or wanted to—get directly involved in during discussions with the parents of prospective students.

None of us ever tried to make the parents feel guilty of self-indulgence, of neglecting their children, or of having a distorted value scale. Once parents are aware of Collegiate's benefits, we leave them alone to think. I can't offer absolute proof, but I have a sneaking suspicion that in the privacy of many homes there has been much discussion and soul-searching over how much a good independent education is worth "sacrificing" for.

I can describe one example because it concerned a fellow working in my business. We had talked about education and he admitted that Collegiate would do a better job of educating his children than the public schools. But, he explained, the school's tuition was beyond his economic means.

I left the discussion at that. A few months later he invited me to his house to listen to his new stereo system. It was very impressive and, out of curiosity, I asked if he minded telling me how much it cost. He didn't, and said $3000. Hmmmmmm, I wondered aloud, how much education would that have bought?

I have no idea what went on in his household after I made that remark. What I do know is that by the next semester he had all three of his children enrolled at Collegiate.

Once they make the decision to come to Collegiate, parents become fantastically demanding—just as if they had bought a new automobile and went back to the dealer for service at the least sign of trouble. They want to make sure that Collegiate's service is first-class and that the school honors its obligations to the paying customers.

The demands may cause a few headaches for the headmaster and faculty, but this is just the way the producer-consumer relationship should be in the market situation. One parent may say, "You're not spending enough time with my slow-learning child," while another would complain, "You're spending too much time with the slow-learners." The headmaster and teachers have to keep everyone happy. They must respect the needs and wants of every parent and student and furnish top-rate service on an equal basis. Otherwise, the customers will think they

55

are not getting their money's worth. Collegiate had to work up to the point where the parent-customer felt that his tuition, whether $600 or $1600, was all service—that every cent went to help his child. Parents paying directly for education can see precisely where their money is going, and how the school spends its income.

Collegiate customers scrutinize the school budget more carefully than public school parents do, and if they think something is wrong they can act immediately to set things straight. It is virtually impossible for a taxpayer to tell where his dollars are going or to do anything if they are going into the wrong places.

Parental budget-scrutiny has put a good deal of helpful pressure on Collegiate. Parents who have had children in public schools enjoy the experience of having control over what they spend on education. If they think that a large percentage of their tuition is being spent on buildings or to support a football team, they won't like it—even if they recognize the need for buildings and sports. The parents must believe, and Collegiate's operating personnel must convince them, that the tuition price being paid is the price of a good education in Wichita, Kansas.

Collegiate's tuition fee is based upon what we have found to be the figure that the market will bear. In any market operation, it is not the costs which determine the price, but what people will pay. When you buy an antique chair, the price does not represent its original construction cost; it represents the current market value of the particular chair.

This is a logical extension of the basic market mechanism wherein the producer or supplier has something that the consumer needs or wants. Once this relationship is established, the price is settled as the producer determines how much the consumer will pay and the consumer finds out for how little the producer will sell.

Our goal was to make Collegiate School financially independent by charging full-cost tuition. We could not do this in the very early days, however. If Collegiate had begun by charging its comparatively few parents a tuition fee covering all operating costs, the majority of parents could not have afforded the high rate and the school would have been deserted. Collegiate charged an amount parents could pay and, despite efforts to keep costs down, suffered deficits until enrollment increased.

Another school, operating in an area where market demand is intense, could succeed in charging full-cost tuition from the outset. By proceeding the way Collegiate did, the school was able to remain in business and earn enough in later years to pay off the debts incurred when tuition and other financing were inadequate.

As Collegiate increased its enrollment, the operating personnel managed to keep down costs by maintaining maximum efficiency. Consequently, the school's tuition has increased comparatively little over a twelve-year period, far less than tuition increases at most colleges, universities, and private schools during the same time. Tuition in the upper school has gone up about $400 and in the lower school, where the market demand is greater, it has risen $600.

Twelve years of experience have shown Collegiate's trustees, headmaster, and faculty where the market is, what it wants in terms of education service, and what it will pay in tuition to get this. The school still suffers from a lack of contrast with other independent educational institutions and where the school has had competition, the effect has been beneficial.

A few years ago several Montessori schools opened in Wichita, competing with the Montessori facilities Collegiate offers in its preschool, kindergarten, and first grade. The new schools charged a price that was some $200 less than we were asking, and Collegiate lowered its tuition to meet the competition and prevent our customers from leaving. After a year of this, realizing that the other schools could not match Collegiate's program, we increased the tuition to the previous rate and were overwhelmed with applicants. Nobody knew what a high-caliber Montessori school Collegiate had until the others came to town. Then the customers could compare and we came out looking very good.

When competition is available and working, the market can function at its best. A monopoly, where new competitors are discouraged and where prices rise continuously while quality deteriorates, frustrates competition and retards development of product quality. Everyone who has ever been involved with Collegiate School will agree with the statement that "The more independent schools there are in Wichita, the better Collegiate's education will be."

In the absence of true competition, Collegiate has had to concentrate all the more on developing the quality of its education product. Like any sound business, Collegiate prospered as its reputation was established. It took years for this to happen, years to gain the confidence of potential customers in the community and to maintain this confidence.

As the school's reputation as a purveyor of educational services improved, we introduced curriculum, teaching, and scheduling innovations, and generally incorporated any sound ideas we came across. We saw that different people in the city were observing the school for different reasons: some liked the language program, others the math curriculum, etc. The customers were starting to take a marketplace view toward education, looking at the different items Collegiate had to offer and comparing these to the public school's inventory.

When the first senior classes graduated and went to college, their performance confirmed the reputation for academic excellence. Today this is the school's strongest selling point. The Collegiate graduates are our best salesmen and their cumulative college record convinces prospective parents of the school's high quality.

The result is that parents now accept Collegiate entirely on its merits. They do not know about the early struggles and community animosity, and probably would not care if they did know. They look at Collegiate's record and like what they see. The contrast that does exist with other Wichita schools has become so great that parents are much more willing to pay the full-cost tuition and count the money they have already unwillingly paid in taxes as a dead loss.

7

Production, or How to Divide Labor and Multiply Efficiency

ANY BUSINESS expecting its income to cover all operating costs cannot afford to be wasteful. At Collegiate School, where the "production department" consists of the trustees, headmaster, and faculty, maximum efficiency was attained by abolishing superfluous positions and establishing a sharply defined division of labor.

In a business, division of labor should equal efficiency. Each component part in the market mechanism knows his job, has the expertise to perform well, and is free to perform as long as the customer is satisfied. There is no waste of time, energy, or money.

Equally important, each element in a division of labor knows what *not* to do, knows where his job ends and another's begins. Overlapping duties are eliminated and authority is specifically assigned and understood.

The Board of Trustees

An executive board—of trustees, directors, or whatever —can help or hinder a business. It depends on who the members are and their attitude toward the business.

The duties of an executive board are to set broad policy and operating philosophy, and to assume ultimate financial responsibility. This is a relatively simple division of labor, as all three duties are interrelated: policy grows out of the philosophy of those who have invested in the business, and to be successful this investment must be backed up by financial commitment.

The executive board's first job is to hire the best chief operating officer it can find, and then leave him alone to run the business. The chief executive is on the scene day after day and is the man most familiar with the business. The board members, who are not present daily, should be smart enough to know they cannot see the business situation through the officer's eyes. The futility of trying to do so reminds me of the story about two men who were put in a room with a solitary fly. One of the men was given a fly-swatter and the other was instructed to tell the first every move to make in order to kill the fly. The fly finally died of old age.

It is impossible for one man, much less a group, to direct another in his duties. Unfortunately, this lesson has not been universally absorbed in business, education, or government. At Collegiate we tried to give maximum freedom to our chief operating officer, the headmaster. If we had one unwritten commandment in our Board of Trustees' meetings it was: *Hands off the headmaster.*

The independence extended to the operating personnel must apply especially to the budgeting process. A board of directors cannot tell the chief operating officer how to prepare a budget any more than it can engineer the death of a fly. It *should* have veto power over the budget, because the board is responsible for making up deficits. The board must insist that the operating officer cut back his expenditures when there are deficits, and if deficits continue the board should think about hiring a new man. The freedom and time given the chief executive to prove himself does not include running the business into bankruptcy.

Collegiate School never went bankrupt, but we did have deficits for several years after we first began. When losses occurred, the trustees put in extra capital of their own. This capital served the same purpose as the reserve fund any young business has on hand to cover unexpected expenses. Supplying reserve capital was part of our board's responsibility, part of its role in the division of labor.

Not every member assumed this responsibility, and consequently I learned that a board such as Collegiate started with is not the best kind to have in an educational institution. The original *raison d'être* for the Collegiate Board of Trustees was to broaden our base of support. Several parents who were prominent in the community were persuaded to serve, with the idea that their presence would help in raising funds for the school. This is similar to the function executive boards fulfill in charitable organizations and some other private schools. Not knowing any better, we went ahead on this basis.

The board never worked in the way it was intended. Our mistake was in thinking even for a moment that this school should be treated as a charitable organization, financed by donations. We quickly learned that if Collegiate were to succeed it had to be run as a business; there was no other way.

The few members of our board who really cared about the school did all the work; those who were only passing time until their children graduated avoided their responsibilities. (Once the school was prospering, of course, some of those who hadn't lifted a finger were suddenly very interested in Collegiate. This did little to enhance my opinion of our Board of Trustees arrangement.)

The same situation is found frequently in other institutions, including businesses. All new organizations want broad support and financial help, and the leaders believe, as we did, that an impressive list of directors is a convenient shortcut to this end. And invariably, the few who are committed to the organization wind up running it.

Whoever controls the financial reins of an organization will in effect "control" the whole show. The broad support that will determine the organization's success comes through pleasing customers, not through having prominent people cajole their friends into donating some spare change.

The simple way to avoid Collegiate's board situation is careful selection. The board of directors, of trustees, or whatever, should be comprised at the outset of those who have committed themselves to the organization's success. This group assumes responsibility for making sure the organization does not fail because of deficits, poor management, or any other factor it can prevent. The members may still make mistakes, may exercise poor judgment, may lose their shirts. But it is their responsibility, no one else's.

There are practical reasons why the operating personnel, especially in a school, should want a board of this type. The law requires that there be tangible evidence of ownership somewhere in the business and, also, lending institutions insist on a personal signature from someone who is responsible and who will remain interested in the borrower's fortunes. It is better for the school employees that the legal owners of its assets, or its loan signatories, are people committed to the school and working actively for its success. (Ideally a school should be owned outright by the headmaster and the faculty. This would define the division of labor even more sharply by having those who raise and spend the money accept ultimate financial responsibility as well, eliminating the necessity for an executive board of any type.)

No matter how it is constituted, the executive board of an independent school bears no relationship to the board of education found in public school systems. When public schools run into financial trouble, the one thing the Board of Education does *not* do is supply the needed capital itself. The usual solution is to increase local taxes, or to ask the federal government for more money or, as a possible last resort, to cut the school budget. But when the budget is cut, the board members have so little understanding of education and such a limited vested interest in the school operation, that cuts are made in the wrong places and the educational product suffers. Because the board members are not personally accountable for the public school system's finances, there is no reason to expect them to act responsibly toward the taxpayers, the teachers, or the students.

Collegiate School's Board of Trustees may have its faults, but at least the members accept personal responsibility for the school's financing. We represent no one but ourselves. When we make mistakes—figure costs wrong, underestimate the number of enrollees, have too many dropouts—it is up to us to close the gap. Nor does Collegiate's Board of Trustees resemble a public school board in its relationship with the operating personnel—

the headmaster and, especially, the faculty. The general rule in public schools, at least in my experience, is for the faculty and the Board of Education to be deadly enemies, at odds over salaries, curriculum, teaching load, *ad infinitum*.

This has not been the case at Collegiate. The majority of trustees have always been parents with children attending the school at the time, and the others parents of recent Collegiate graduates. In addition to having a financial commitment to the school, then, trustees serving on Collegiate's board have treated the faculty in a manner that would be helpful to their children. No trustee ever wanted his children singled out for special treatment, whether favorable or unfavorable. We would think twice about some criticism we might have about a teacher. We did not want to interfere in their relationship with their students. The atmosphere of cooperation and mutual respect which resulted has been very healthy for the growth of the school.

No matter how well intentioned an executive board may be, each member must always be ready to spot another member who is growing suspicious or angry over something happening in a classroom. Unless he is calmed down, this trustee will likely start thinking of all the money, time, and energy he has put into the school and be anxious to step in and "take care of things" himself. If a board member does start meddling in the classroom and nobody stops him, you have trouble.

The Collegiate board has been fortunate to include enough committed, involved members who are aware of what is happening at the school and can sense when trouble is brewing. At our board meetings we repeat again and again the idea that our concern is broad policy *only*.

Our duty is to take a long-range view of the school and resolve any unexpected crises in this light, and this attitude pertains to our relationship with the headmaster and faculty as well as to parents and students. Whenever a trustee has become upset over something, we have asked ourselves whether or not the overall situation was sufficiently favorable to counteract the immediate unfortunate "crisis."

There have been many cases where I personally did not particularly like the headmaster's final decision, or the way a teacher handled a situation. But I had to look at the matter as I would my conduct toward my company's personnel: if somebody is profitable to the business and making progress, and then makes a mistake, the question to be asked is, how many *right* decisions has he made? If an employee is making most of his decisions correctly, he is no doubt a reliable, productive man and in this light, this particular mistake is tolerable.

The only way operating personnel can make a business successful is if the board of directors or the owner gives them the freedom and the time to be successful. If they do not succeed, and the fault is indisputably theirs, then and only then should the board or owner step in and make replacements. The same rule applies to a school.

The Headmaster

The most important man in an educational institution, no matter who is putting up the money, is the headmaster. He is the chief operating officer; indeed he is the only one. He must be educator and public relations man, recruiting officer and accountant, diplomat and taskmaster; he must make his budget and live with it, he must hire the faculty

67

and live with them. A good headmaster has to be a super-man, yet not be so vain as to act like one.

Considering the scope of the headmaster's duties, and the pressures he gets from parents, students, and teachers, it is understandable why the executive board has to leave him alone to do his job. The best executive in the world cannot work with someone else on his back all the time. He must have freedom in his job and adequate time to prove himself.

This "proving period" should not last forever, of course. There is no pat rule-of-thumb as to when the executive board should replace its chief operating officer, but a board that is truly involved will be able to tell when the leadership begins to lag. When a school stops progressing and starts living off the assets it has built up over the years, it's time for the board to take a long, hard look at the chief officer.

Collegiate School has had two headmasters during its twelve-year existence. The first resigned for personal reasons after three years and the second has been with the school ever since. I am convinced that a major reason the school is successful today is because the headmaster was kept on long enough and given the freedom to prove himself and his program.

When our second headmaster was getting started there were occasions when some parent or trustee would raise the cry that he should be bounced. I had reason to question a few of his decisions myself and the two of us had several toe-to-toe discussions over just what his plans were.

But whenever any of this dissatisfaction surfaced, there was always a calming voice on the board to remind us that our job was to look at the overall picture. We were young and inexperienced in the education business, and had to ask ourselves constantly if we knew enough to jump in every time we thought we saw something wrong. Needless to say, the board backed the headmaster 100 percent of the time.

The trustees had a lot to learn about running an educational institution and the headmaster had a lot to learn about running a business. When we were recruiting a headmaster, we found that there was virtually nobody available in the field of private education who held the view that a school is a business where income covers operating costs. The few who maintained this principle already ran their own schools.

The prevalent idea among headmasters we talked to was that they were only to administer the school, that the financial problems were the province of the trustees. The headmasters wanted low tuition so they could educate as many students as possible, but they did not want to be held responsible for the low income and deficits which result from low tuition. These were to be covered—somehow—by the trustees.

Collegiate's Board of Trustees realized that deficits were unavoidable in a young business, but we were not about to tolerate a continuous stream of red ink. We were looking for a young, self-motivated headmaster with a good academic background who could operate independently, who was willing to be held accountable for his decisions, and who could be educated into making the school operation financially self-sufficient. This was the broad operating philosophy, established by the Board of Trustees, that the headmaster had to work within.

The headmaster's obligation was to see that income

from tuition matched the school's expenses. He had to learn to make these calculations correctly, and understand that he could not expect the board to cover deficits forever. If an insufficient number of students enrolled in September to cover the headmaster's budget for the school year, the trustees would either have to make up the deficit or shut down the school. Other trustees and I told the headmaster day after day, "You've got to cut your budget and increase your income." If he wanted to have a burgeoning bureaucracy of department heads and so forth, the headmaster could not expect to have an efficient, low-budget operation. He had to eliminate every ounce of waste in the school. Our present headmaster has learned this lesson by doing. Each year for the past nine years he has drawn up a budget that he thought was absolutely bare-boned, and then found places to cut more fat.

The second part of the headmaster's education concerned increasing income. Shortly after our second headmaster went to work he dismissed several students for disciplinary and academic reasons. I told him that the trustees would back him up on the dismissals, and then asked how he planned to make up the lost income. At first he didn't believe it was a serious question. It was. Finally our headmaster learned that we meant what we said about income equaling costs. Now he and the faculty do everything they can for students before dismissing anyone.

The success of an independent school involves a cycle that begins with an efficient operation. Keep the budget down by keeping efficiency up, and productivity will increase and new income will be generated. The more income, the better the operation.

The key to a smoothly functioning operation is an at-

70

mosphere of peace and cooperation. Nothing can destroy an organization quicker than internal strife, factionalism, and bickering. And in the school it is the headmaster, the chief operating officer, who is ultimately responsible for keeping peace with and among parents, students, teachers, and trustees.

The main burden of the headmaster's peace-keeping job is to make sure the customers—the parents—are happy. In twelve years of experience with Collegiate School we have developed some guidelines for accomplishing this. The important consideration is always to treat each parent as a customer who has willingly bought the school's service-product.

Discussions with the parents about problems their children may have in school must be honest and frank. Parents must be reassured that the faculty will provide every service available to correct the problem. Sometimes parents, unable to accept the truth about their children, will be offended by the headmaster's honesty and either try to have him fired or withdraw their youngsters. What happens more often is that the parent, having made the decision to invest a considerable amount of money in his child's education, becomes very demanding of the faculty and its services.

There is no way to foresee the demands parents will make or the conflicts that will arise between parents and teachers, but the headmaster has to be prepared to meet any situation. Our basic rule at Collegiate has always been that academic problems should be settled at the lowest level, in a discussion between the individual teacher and the individual parent (including trustee-parents). If the teacher or the parent should go to the headmaster first, he gets them together with the other party immediately and will intervene only in the unlikely event no solution can be reached at the lower level.

This does not mean the headmaster can just sit back, confident that all complaints and conflicts will be resolved peacefully. He has to know what is going on in the school every minute and cannot afford to be caught off-guard by a conflict that could quickly mushroom into something big.

At Collegiate the headmaster keeps up on developments by teaching two courses. He has continuing, firsthand experience with students in the classrooms, and so can better counsel other teachers on how they might handle a particular problem. Second, he visits classes unannounced. He is not "spying" on the teachers, but simply trying to make sure that he can deal with *parents'* complaints about teachers if they should arise.

This careful day-to-day observation has paid off at Collegiate. On one occasion a group of parents came to the headmaster with some questions about a certain teacher's competence, a matter they could not take up with the teacher directly. Because the headmaster had sat in on a couple of the teacher's classes, he was able to say immediately to the parents, "I know exactly what you're talking about and here's what I have been doing." He then explained how the school was arranging for a tutor to provide the teacher with some auxiliary help until she could handle her class properly. This type of awareness has an immediate calming effect on parents, who might otherwise become increasingly agitated and do great damage to the school.

If the headmaster knows the score in every classroom

it will also help when unresolved problems are brought to him. It is important that both the parent and the teacher think of the headmaster as their champion, making it even more essential that he understand the situation accurately. His final decision may offend either the teacher or the parent to the degree that one of them leaves the school. A political or arbitrary decision would be unjust to all concerned.

The parent-teacher-headmaster conferences can be tricky business. Prior to the conference the teacher has on occasion said one thing to the headmaster concerning the student in question, and then said something completely different when confronted by the child's parents. The headmaster has told the parents what to expect, based on what the teacher has told him earlier. Then when all three get together in one room, and the teacher says, "Oh Johnny's not really that bad a student," the headmaster is in trouble.

There must be mutual trust, honesty, and respect between the headmaster and his faculty. Except for a rare incident like that described above, we have had this at Collegiate. The fact that the headmaster must be highly involved in the total operation, aware of what is going on inside—and outside—the school, has brought him into a closer relationship with the faculty.

The headmaster hires (and fires) individual teachers. He wants them to be productive and please the customers. He doesn't jump all over them the minute a parent complains, any more than the trustees jump on him. He wants the teachers to establish good relations with the customers —the parents and students—but he realizes that, above all, the teachers' job is to teach. Teachers must have the same freedom in their job as the headmaster has in his.

Several times mothers have come to our headmaster and said they would like to have a rummage sale or a bake sale or something of that sort in one of the grades. His reply is always, "Fine, but you mothers do it, don't bother the teacher. If the teacher offers to help, good and well, but her job is to teach, not be a social director." Several of those mothers have been very upset when the headmaster told them that, but he has to do it. He has to protect the teachers from this sort of intrusion.

When the headmaster and a faculty member trust and respect each other, there are no problems when it comes time to negotiating the teacher's contract. This can be done fairly, honestly, and without acrimony and group-bargaining difficulties. The headmaster knows how productive the teacher is, based on what he has observed in the classroom, on what the parents feel, and on what other faculty members have said about the students of that teacher.

The teachers and the headmaster at Collegiate School have a true market relationship. The teachers are negotiating for as high a salary as they can get, which is natural. The headmaster knows how productive teachers are, how much they are worth to the school, and makes his salary offer accordingly. Thus far, we have not had a single teacher resign because of insufficient pay.

The headmaster must judge the value teachers have to the school and then gauge their monetary worth. This is not an exercise in omnipotence, it is simply a fact of business life: somebody judges all of us, how much we are worth to them in dollar terms, or in terms of what must be sacrificed to maintain our allegiance. I judge my employees, my customers judge me.

In any business the chief executive gets the biggest headaches and the biggest pleasures. And he is paid very well for doing his job well.

Collegiate's headmaster can raise his own salary by managing efficiently and eliminating the needs for other administrations. His salary is commensurate with his value to the school as judged by the trustees. Good executives are hard to find, and are in great demand in the job market. If Collegiate's headmaster does a good job, and the trustees want to retain him, they have to make the position lucrative enough so that no one can lure him away.

The Faculty

An independent school has the flexibility to waive teacher-certification requirements and hire faculty members who have something to offer the students and can please the consumer-parents. This is the approach Collegiate's headmaster takes when he considers the question of which teachers to employ.

Teachers are hired to produce a high-quality student. They are given the freedom, resources, and moral and financial support needed to accomplish this. They are an independent unit within Collegiate School's division of labor.

At Collegiate each teacher is fully in charge of an individual "business," so to say—his or her classroom. Collegiate teachers are frequently reminded: "You are independent, you are responsible, you alone run this classroom."

75

Elsewhere in education teachers are increasingly isolated from the parent, surrounded by a buffer system of counselors, principals, vice-principals, vice-presidents, advisers, and so on. At Collegiate, there is nobody but the teacher, the student, and the parent. Most of the teachers have understood what is meant by "independence." It means they can do as they please, and they do. They hand out discipline, set their own rules for classroom decorum, innovate in the curriculum, and teach to each student's potential, working at different levels with the fast, the medium, and the slow learners.

The teachers welcome this atmosphere. It has been more difficult to have teachers understand and accept the responsibilities that go with the independence they like so well. This was especially so during Collegiate's earlier years, when teachers faced with disciplinary or academic problems were inclined to recommend the student's dismissal without themselves attempting to correct the situation.

While the teachers enjoyed their classroom freedom, the school was losing income. They were not yet aware that, in order to maintain their independence, each teacher had to make a concerted effort to help the student and keep him enrolled. Otherwise, too much lost income would eventually mean loss of teaching jobs—and no more freedom.

The teachers, like the headmaster, needed a lesson in the economics of education. And once the headmaster had learned to respect the relationship between costs and income, the faculty members did, too. The headmaster could not very well have an efficient school operation, with a balanced budget every year, if the teachers were not helping to cut costs and increase income. He had to say to the teachers, as the trustees had said to him, "How can we meet the budget if we don't have the students?"

Collegiate teachers received one of their most effective economics lessons as a result of a study conducted to examine the school's expenses. The purpose of the cost study, ordered by the Board of Trustees, was to find out where the school's overhead expenses should be applied to the production process.

The overhead was broken down by grades, so each teacher could see in black and white what portion was incurred by her "business." A first-grade teacher, for example, would be responsible for a percentage of the school's expenses for utilities (heat, light, power), for maintenance, for gymnasium upkeep, for testing facilities, for the library, etc.

If it did nothing else, the cost study compelled the faculty to think of the school operation, and their unit, in terms of total cost. They realized that teachers were accountable for many more expenses than the amount of money spent on books and materials for their students. Nobody had ever presented this to them before.

The cost breakdown was a dramatic way of showing the teachers that every time a student was dismissed or left the school—perhaps because the child's teacher hadn't tried hard enough—it meant x-dollars less that the school had on hand to meet overhead costs. How was this going to be made up? Out of the teachers' salaries? Suddenly the faculty began to look at the school's economics in a new light.

Even when they understood the economics, it took time for all the teachers to make a total effort with each student.

Many of our faculty members have come to Collegiate after teaching in public schools, and they were just not used to giving this kind of attention to the student.

We had to keep impressing upon the teachers the fact that, if they tried twice to get a good performance from a youngster in public school, they should try at least five times at Collegiate. One area of education where Collegiate had to be better than the public schools was in giving more attention to the individual needs of the individual student.

Extra attention meant more work and more patience for the teachers. It is part of the teachers' work assignments, the understanding they have with the headmaster, that they are to give special attention, outside the normal class situation, to every student. The brighter youngsters will be given special learning projects or advanced books to read, and the teacher will continue to work closely with them. With the children who have an academic problem, the teacher will spend time during the day or after school counseling each individually. If this is thought to be insufficient, the teacher will recommend a tutorial program within the school. As a last resort, the teacher will level with the parent and recommend an outside tutor. Sometimes the parents will suggest this, or will offer to pay the teacher for extra tutoring. But Collegiate teachers will do all they can to help the student on their own time, and not increase the cost of education for the parent.

The teachers are also constantly introducing innovations which will give them more time to spend with individual students. We now have computerized teaching machines in several of the upper-school classes—math, languages, English—which allow the students to study on their own and free the teacher for personal counseling. Some of the more advanced classes in math, language, and science have no formal meetings at all, but combine independent study and individual instruction.

The more-patience, more-work ethic pertains to disciplinary as well as academic situations. Collegiate could not continue to function if teachers recommend dismissal every time a student stepped out of line. The teachers had to learn and mature in their independence. They had no choice but to handle disciplinary problems on their own, without bothering the headmaster, offending parents, hurting students, or jeopardizing their own position as director of a "business."

This was a tall order and it did not come easy for every teacher. We had one man who came to Collegiate when he was in his forties, had never taught before, and was, I think, a bit nervous that students might get the best of him. Whenever he had a rowdy incident in his class he would hand out disciplinary slips to everyone involved, and the recipients had to go to the school on Saturday and work.

It happened that this same teacher had agreed to oversee the school's landscaping and he had to use some of his own disciplinary cases to help him on weekends. One day he came to me in a state of total frustration. "I've had it with this forced labor on Saturdays. They just won't do a good job," he complained. And I had to say to him, "Well, you teach economics and you know that slavery is uneconomical. It shouldn't be any surprise to you."

This teacher didn't hand out any discipline slips after that day. He learned that force doesn't work. Patience, work, and cooperation are far more productive than arbitrary punishment, even if you do have to reprimand kids from time to time.

The economic health of Collegiate depended on the teachers having good relations with the parents as well as the students. Often the two go together. Our faculty members are constantly calling in the parents of their students for a talk and making themselves available whenever a parent wishes to talk to them. Having mastered the concept of producer-consumer relationships, the teachers treat the parents as the paying customers they are.

This can occasionally be a very delicate role for the teacher. The classroom teacher will sometimes tell the parents things about their child that the parents don't want to hear. On one occasion the nephew of a trustee was told by his teacher that he was going to have to buckle down and work his senior year if he expected to graduate. His parents thought the teacher was being unfair. They tried to have the trustee intercede but he refused. Later the trustee found that what the teacher had said was the absolute truth—the boy hadn't been doing his work. The parents never did accept the evidence, and had the youngster transferred to a private school out of town.

In another case, the teacher simply recommended that the parents get outside tutoring help for their child. The teacher had done all she could and thought more help was needed. This has been suggested on several occasions at Collegiate with no problems. This time, however, the student's mother objected and accused the teacher of "giving up" on her child. She removed her children from Collegiate and sent them to public schools. I think this type of reaction is self-destructive, but it happens and the teacher has to be ready for it.

The teachers get pressure from all sides. One set of parents may say, "If you do so-and-so we're leaving school," and another set will say, "If you *don't* do so-and-so we're leaving." And I know how the parents feel. I was one, too, not long ago.

I'll admit that there were times when I had to hold back from complaining that a teacher was spending time with other students and not enough with my own children. I forced myself to see this as the selfish negative attitude it was. Only in a one-to-one classroom situation can each student receive maximum teacher attention. The proper question is: How much attention *are* my children getting and is this the most possible?

Generally, Collegiate teachers are on excellent terms with "their" parents. It is a part of their job in the division of labor and keeps the production cycle running smoothly. For their part, most parents make a point of getting to know the teacher and following their child's educational development very closely. They want to see where the money's going.

In the spring of 1971 the school developed a plan combining the teacher's responsibilities of keeping tuition income up and maintaining good relations with parents. In simple terms, the faculty members were put in charge of student recruitment. They solicited the parents directly, asking them to re-enroll their children.

This was a very radical departure for teachers to take. We were reducing the producer-consumer relationship to its basic level, with the producer drumming up patronage for his product by using virtual door-to-door salesmanship.

The new recruiting program was a great success the first time it was tried. The teachers got to know the parents better and the parents were even more aware of the teachers' attitude toward them as customers. Each party was making a commitment to the child's education in the immediate presence of the other, and this improved parent-teacher relationships throughout the following school year.

A teacher who is able to be productive, to keep students enrolled and make parents happy, is going to be paid very well. Our faculty members know that they are continually being judged—by students, parents, headmaster, and other teachers—on the basis of their production quality and that their reputation rides on every class that leaves their grade or course.

That reputation spreads and is known to everyone. Parents with children coming up through the school know exactly what the next teacher's reputation is, and if the teacher hasn't been producing, the parents will ask questions before enrolling their children in the class. They don't want to invest a lot of money in a dubious producer.

Obviously, a teacher who has produced twenty happy students and twenty sets of happy parents and has an efficient, smooth-running "business" operation is going to be in a very strong bargaining position with the headmaster. The teachers know that Collegiate is trying to keep costs down by paying attractive wages to the best people and that those teachers who are hired have a high market value. This is why there are no formal, binding teachers' contracts at Collegiate. The school really wants to keep its good teachers, and the headmaster tries to make the learning atmosphere pleasant enough for the teacher to want to teach there. If a teacher should ever decide to leave in the middle of a term, he or she is free to go. We could not and would not want to prevent a departure. Forcing a teacher to stay creates an unpleasant situation on all sides.

The school has to trust the teachers in this regard, and the teachers have to trust the school. There have been only three cases in twelve years of teachers being dismissed in the middle of the year, and these were all exceptional cases (one fellow did little in his English class except tell dirty jokes). And virtually the only reason a teacher will be dismissed at the end of the year is if either the parents or the headmaster believe the school can hire someone better, more productive.

Collegiate isn't interested, however, in playing "musical chairs" with its teachers. It hires instructors with the intention of having them develop and grow and achieve excellence, not to replace them a year or two later with somebody else. When teachers do develop in this way, so their financial value increases in like manner.

One of the questions I am asked most frequently about Collegiate School is, "How do your teachers' salaries compare with those in public schools?" Public school salary schedules change so often that I can never be absolutely sure of the answer. I do know that our salaries are substantially higher for experienced teachers, and that beginning teachers reach the higher level as soon as they are actually productive and not when some salary schedule says they are ready. As an example, we recently hired a young fellow who wasn't quite sure he wanted to be a full-time teacher. He started out at $250 a month as a part-timer in the humanities program. After a couple of months he had grown to like the job, wanted to teach full time, and had his salary changed to $6,000 a year. By the end of the next school year his salary was up to $7,500.

Even if an independent school cannot match public

sector salaries down the line, it offers teachers so many other advantages that a strictly monetary comparison is misleading. There is the individual freedom in the classroom, of course, and also the flexibility in the curriculum, the opportunity to experiment with students, teaching methods, and course materials. Another consideration is the fact that Collegiate students are the children of parents who are at least interested enough in the child's education to pay for it directly. These students are not attending Collegiate because they *have* to. How much is this worth to a teacher?

Finally, Collegiate's faculty is the most essential unit in its division of labor. They are treated accordingly, in terms of salary as well as in the respect and consideration they are afforded by others associated with the school. When teachers are not treated in this manner, when they are abused, a school's production won't be worth a damn.

The Bureaucracy

The bureaucracy at Collegiate School consists of the headmaster and his secretary. No educational institution of this size needs any more. Additional "administrators" would be useless and a waste of valuable money. I wonder if this isn't true for much larger academic institutions.

To the people of Collegiate School this need for a wage economy and the means to achieve it appear simple and logical. It is not so easy for others to understand, especially when the "others" work in a situation where the bureaucracy is already in bloom.

An associate of mine was approached a few years ago by representatives of a small Kansas college, and was told that the school was thinking about implementing the full-cost pricing philosophy. The representative invited him to discuss the subject with the school's trustees, and upon arrival he was ushered into a conference room and introduced to those present. Among them were the college president, vice-president, dean of men, and director of development.

These four "administrators," my associate guessed, were costing the school an average of $25,000 a year, each with a secretary and a private office. This added up to $100,-000-plus in wasted overhead at a college having only 100 or so more students than Collegiate. The first question he was asked by one of the four bureaucrats was, "How do we go about putting full-cost pricing into effect?" It was all my friend could do to keep from laughing.

Bureaucracies have a way of growing completely on their own. They feed on themselves and their growth bears no relation to the conditions surrounding them. Once created, the bureaucracy becomes entrenched, as much a part of the institutional environment as the furniture. Each of the four bureaucrats at this small college undoubtedly thought he was vitally important to the school's well-being. Who was around to disagree?

One of the remarkable things about bureaucracies is that the employees they hurt most, those below who cannot move without a bureaucrat's say-so, seldom complain about the lack of trust and independence. Bureaucracies are very good at insulating people from the real world. Their endurance is directly related to the number of hands they can hold and worried brows they can soothe. The bureaucracy becomes the employee's protector and confessor, and as this arrangement is comforting to both bureaucrat and worker, no one is concerned over lost efficiency.

This seems especially to be the case in public schools. While some teachers may complain from time to time about the red tape and administrative bungling, they would rather put up with this than get rid of all the counselors, principals, and other administrators who absorb all the heat and insulate the faculty as they bounce around in the middle, between superintendent and teacher. The parents are left talking to middle-level bureaucrats who have no responsibility to them.

Probably the worst effect an entrenched bureaucracy can have is the example it sets for younger institutions in the same field. Everybody simply has to have a bureaucracy he can call his own. It is a prerequisite for success.

This, I'm afraid, is what happens in education. The public schools (including publicly owned colleges) are top-heavy with bureaucracies—and young private schools usually follow suit.

This also happened at Collegiate—or almost happened. At one point we had a head of the lower school, several department heads, and a dean for the men and the women. It was only a matter of time before this would have expanded to include an upper-school head, a director of curriculum, of admissions, or dismissals, or transportation, of sidewalks, windows, doors, and so on.

The reason Collegiate had any bureaucracy to begin with was the influence of the public schools. If we had two faculty members teaching the same subject, one of them had to be the "department head"—and receive extra pay for the "administrative" work—because this was the way it was done in public schools.

86

We should have known better. No businessman would tolerate this sort of inefficiency in his business, and the Board of Trustees had to learn to apply the same standards to Collegiate. Inefficiency is inefficiency, wherever it exists. I later recalled that a manager in my company had once asked me to hire someone to "coordinate" two jobs in his division. My immediate reaction was to tell the fellow he was fired. Naturally, he asked why. "Because," I explained, "when you get things so screwed up that you need somebody around to 'coordinate' you out of a mess, it doesn't speak too well for your executive ability." He saw the light and no coordinator was hired.

Eventually Collegiate's trustees came to see that "administrators" in a school are no different from "coordinators" in a business. They are useless, unnecessary handmaidens to weak people. Our first skepticism about school bureaucrats was prompted by their cost. After we suffered deficits for two straight years, the trustees sat down with the headmaster to see where costs could be cut some more. When we came to the expense for "administrators" we had to ask the same question applied to every cost: "Why?"

The headmaster answered that the school needed somebody for parents to complain to. Eureka! Why wasn't the teacher the person the complaints went to? Most often the teacher is directly involved with whatever is causing the complaint, so why not have the parent and teacher talk it out?

Understanding the concept of each teacher being in charge of his or her own little "business" led us to further understanding of the educational process. It confirmed our belief that the basic academic relationship is that among parent, student, and teacher, and that the headmaster should push the heat he gets from parents back onto the teacher if that is where it belongs. This affords the headmaster more time to perform any real administrative duties, making additional bureaucrats all the more unnecessary.

As Collegiate grew larger, the school personnel made it a point to stick to original principles. The usual trend in our bureaucrat-oriented society is for the decision-making process to get more complicated the larger an institution becomes. When one level of management breaks down, another level is superimposed on top to "coordinate" the confusion. This trend is insane. It is just the opposite of what should be done. As an institution grows larger and more complex, the less the people on top are going to know about what's happening below. The people who do know the score below are those working there. They are the ones who should make decisions affecting their level. Everyone else should keep hands off.

Collegiate grew larger and more complex over the years, and the headmaster found he could make fewer and fewer informed decisions. He wasn't stupid or lazy, just realistic. The school operation was too large for him to know all the facts in a situation at a lower level. The teachers at that level have more facts, and the decisions are left to them. If the decision turns out to be wrong, they have to live with it.

As Collegiate School grew, so did the freedom and independence of the units within its division of labor.

8

Finances, or The Fine Art of
Full-Cost Pricing

THE HISTORY OF Wichita Collegiate School is
one of identifying costs, minimizing them without sacrificing the educational quality, and charging a
tuition rate at least high enough to cover all operating
costs. This economic philosophy is called full-cost pricing:
income from the established price at least equals the full
cost incurred in production.

The keystone of this process is the budget, the annual
tally of cold hard figures showing what the school wants
to do and what it has to do it with. Budget-making under
the full-cost pricing system is a fine art. It required long
years of practice for us to get to the point where every
item in the "expenditures" column was matched in the
"income" column.

Whoever is preparing and living with such a budget
places himself up against the wall. His financial backers
may underwrite some deficits, but not forever. He has to
cut costs continually and raise the income. And, although
costs can be cut, the quality of the product cannot be lowered, as that is what he is "selling." This is the financial

dilemma Collegiate School has experienced, and which any independent school wishing to be self-sufficient must also experience.

The Budget

There is no mystery or magic in the way the headmaster prepares the budget at Collegiate School. First, he decides what services the school will offer during the next school year. Second, he determines what these services will cost. Third, he estimates the number of students who will enroll for the next year. Fourth, he sets a tuition figure that will cover the service costs. The fifth step, though not a part of the budget preparation, is that the headmaster be sure the school recruits enough students, at the tuition price he has set, to bring in the actual cash to pay all the costs.

There is treacherous ground between the first step and the last. If the student enrollment is below the headmaster's estimate, or if he has misjudged service costs, the school is going to end up in the red. Over 90 percent of Collegiate's expenses are fixed costs that will remain unchanged whether the school has forty students or four hundred. The headmaster's calculations have to be on target or the whole school will sink into bankruptcy.

The usual situation in most private—as well as public—schools is for the headmaster to draw up a budget, project enrollment, and then hand the whole matter over to the executive board. Headmasters in this situation are not responsible for the budget they prepare. When a deficit occurs, and one usually does, the board is expected either to raise the needed money or to withdraw the needed money from the school's endowment.

Headmasters have boasted to me that "Our tuition only

pays fifty percent of our costs," as if financial irresponsibility were a badge of honor. When I ask them what their biggest problem is, most of them say, "Lack of money." Amazing. Many of these same schools cater to the moneyed elite whose sons so often become public office-holders—in case you ever wondered where our government leaders get their earliest economic "education."

Collegiate has had its share of financial problems, its poorly prepared budgets, enrollment miscalculations, deficits, trustee "investments." But the people at Collegiate tried to learn from these mistakes, and we were all consciously working toward the goal of making the school financially self-sufficient.

When Collegiate's present headmaster arrived, he was no more eager to accept full responsibility for the school's costs than any other private school headmaster would have been. He balked at undertaking the nitty-gritty work of balancing income against expenditures. One solution would have been to fire that headmaster and find one who would unhesitatingly accept the financial responsibility. Instead, the trustees agreed to accept the initial deficits as capital expenditures and impressed on the headmaster the fact that he had to cut the budget and increase income. And he, in turn, had to persuade the faculty to help hold down expenses and produce new income.

Gradually, the tide began to turn, income and expenses were balanced, and Collegiate managed to reverse the tendency frequently found in other nonpublic schools: each year the school's budget was reduced, not expanded. If student enrollment did not go up at the same time, at least the reduced expenditures kept the deficit lower than it would have been otherwise.

When enrollment and income did increase, and the costs were still coming down, Collegiate was finally in a solvent position. The school then started paying off old debts and could consider the luxury of banking surplus income.

An enterprise like Collegiate School, especially a young enterprise, will have two categories of expenses in its budget. One will be the operating costs—what it takes to run the school physically. The other will be the capital—money that either has been or will be invested in new buildings, equipment, and other major items.

I have always contended that capital expenditures should be included in Collegiate's general budget along with the operating costs, and that earnings should cover both. While this is not done at most other educational institutions, it is the way capital expenditures are handled in any business. If my company borrows a million dollars, we immediately add the interest and a percentage of the repayment to our budget. "Why should Collegiate be any different," I asked politely.

This was one time I didn't get my way. The other trustees wanted to keep the capital separate, wait a few years, and then have a "drive" among the school's financial backers to cover the indebtedness. I reluctantly went along, knowing that none of these trustees would run a business on such a slipshod basis. They were thinking with their hearts, not their heads.

After a couple of years went by, I brought up the subject of our debts and asked, "When are we going to have that fund drive?" And somebody replied, "Great idea, Bob, why don't you lead it?" So I led the drive. And I made the first contribution, as I was not about to ask somebody to do something I wasn't ready to do myself. Then three or four other trustees put up some cash, and that was all. The rest were in hiding, guarding their checkbooks or pleading poverty. The argument to keep capital separate and pay for it with a special-fund drive turned out to be a big joke. The same thing happened when it was necessary to mortgage the school buildings in order to complete construction and pay the total bill. Only the same small group of trustees was willing to sign the mortgage notes and assume responsibility for whatever happened to the school. The others knew they should sign, some said they really wanted to, but for various personal reasons they did not make the final commitment.

There are only two sources of capital: earnings and gifts. At Collegiate the idea of depending on gift contributions was discarded. My position all along was that covering capital expenditures with earnings is the dependable, stable way to operate.

I don't have anything against donating money to a school, and have done so myself on several occasions. There are, however, good reasons why the school's operating personnel must be cautious of gift horses, always looking them straight in the mouth. One is that gifts come with strings attached.

Collegiate's position on this matter was that the school would accept a financial gift as long as the "strings" would not force it to compromise or alter in any way the curriculum, teaching methods, grading system, personnel, or other educational operations. If a donor wanted a building named after him, or built with a red roof, and the school needed the structure, it took the money and started construction. That was the only type of "string" with which Collegiate ever became tied.

This question of need is another reason why a school must be wary of gifts and gift-givers. Nothing could be more suicidal for a young school than to have a donor finance a new building and then find it did not have the additional operating cash required to keep the building open.

This situation is analogous to the fellow who wins a Cadillac on a TV quiz show and then has to turn and sell it immediately because he can't afford the insurance, gas, and oil. If a school needs a new classroom building or gymnasium and a donor is willing to finance it, fine. But the trustees must beware of Mr. Fatwallet and his dream of a Fatwallet Memorial Bottle Cap Museum that is going to cost the school a bundle in overhead.

There was one more argument I used in trying to have capital expenses included in the general budget: the fact that if the school were not totally self-sufficient, gifts could rule its direction. A school is most vulnerable, I argued, when it has to look outside its earnings for money to operate. The right man with the right amount of money could come along at the right time and take over the school.

I had already done this at Collegiate, so I knew what I was talking about. And if I did it, so could somebody else. My commitment to Collegiate was strong enough that I wanted to help improve the school's financial position to the point where I could no longer be influential solely because of my financial backing. If this could be done, I felt confident that no one else could step in later and do what I had done.

I have seen what happens at private schools where headmasters boast of tuition covering only 50 percent of the costs. Earnings are inadequate, money is needed to meet operating expenses, and the schools turn to wealthy trustees, alumni, or parents. Consequently, these potential donors are courted and pampered by the school administrators and faculty while the majority of parents (and students) take a place at the end of the line. Gifts rule the school's budget and the givers rule the school.

The federal government is now teaching the same lesson to local school boards all across the nation. Federal funds constitute less than 10 percent of the total budget of the Wichita public schools, but the system cannot function without this money, small percentage though it is. The government is able, therefore, to dictate school policy. In business we would consider that to be "good leverage."

I knew that if Collegiate became self-sufficient, with a truly broad base of support, the teachers and headmaster would not have to bow down to anybody who made a big donation. Parents would be paying their own way, in identical amounts at each grade level, and the school would be free to treat each customer equally. The customer who pays hundreds of dollars each year for his child's education deserves all the consideration a school can give. The parent who happens also to be rich deserves no more for his child than the one who is poor. That is the only way it should be.

After a few years of my harping on the subject of self-sufficiency, the trustees finally changed their ways and Collegiate gradually began to incorporate its capital expenditures into the general operating budget. We had incurred some debts when the school had its deficits, and these had been signed for and carried almost ten years on somebody's good credit. The first thing included in the Collegiate budget from the capital column was the interest on the old debts, and then the principal. Over four or five years the school was able to wipe out its old debts and move over to the type of budget that has only one set of figures—operating costs.

Now, if the headmaster wants to buy some new equipment, he puts the item in his budget for the next year and knows where the money is coming from to finance it. The school operation is run entirely on tuition earnings, and Collegiate has not had a deficit since 1966.

Collegiate's operating expenses include only the costs of keeping the physical plant running and of educating children. These operating expenses represent the budget area where the headmaster has to scrutinize every item year after year, and include utilities, maintenance, salaries, equipment, and teaching materials. They cannot be eliminated, only reduced. We have made cost studies at the school, identifying every penny in overhead and where it was spent, to help the headmaster guard against waste and inefficiency.

The headmaster will build a margin of error into the budget to cover unforeseen expenses or protect against a sudden drop off in enrollment. At the start of the 1971-72 school year Collegiate discovered it would have to buy a bus of its own. The company we had been renting from told the school that all of its vehicles would be needed to help implement the busing plan in Wichita public schools. The cushion in the budget allowed the school to go ahead and buy a bus without having to depend on a gift, loan, or parental assessment.

The way Collegiate's budget is now prepared, if only 80 percent of the estimated enrollment shows up in September, the school's operating costs will be covered. Then, if the entire 100 percent does appear, the headmaster will have a cushion.

This margin of error is comfortable to have and any independent school operating under the full-cost pricing philosophy would be wise to include this in its budget. To be effective, however, the margin must be treated realistically. The fact that actual operating costs could be covered by only 75 or 80 percent of the projected total income does not mean that the enrollment or tuition figures should be lowered 20 or 25 percent. Instead, the school should try for a surplus of income. This can be used, first, to pay off old debts, and then be applied to new capital expenditures, the scholarship program, or banked to protect the school and its customers against future economic reversals. Treated in this manner, the margin of error serves as an inspiration to cut costs even further.

Controlling Costs

In the early days of Collegiate School, controlling the operating and capital costs was a matter of necessity. We could not afford to do otherwise. In the last ten years, Collegiate's financial position has improved greatly, but the cost-consciousness has stayed with us. In fact, the headmaster is even tougher at cutting the budget today— he's had more experience.

Whenever a teacher requisitions some new materials, or a new activity is proposed, the first question is still, "How are we going to pay for it?" Just because the school has more financial strength does not mean Parkinson's Law automatically goes into effect and our costs should expand to meet the revenue available.

Collegiate's approach to cost control has been to break the total school operation down into the smallest individual economic units: the classroom, the course, the activity. The costs of each, including percentage of overhead, are compared against the income each unit produces. If the costs are too high, they have to be lowered, or more income must be produced. Should neither solution work, the unit must either be reduced in scope or eliminated.

The school's ultimate goal is to have each of its several units functioning autonomously. In a classroom this means having the ideal enrollment of twenty students and keeping costs at a level where they can be covered by tuition income. In such optional activities as lunch, transportation, and athletics it means charging participants a price that will cover materials and overhead costs.

Gifts can be useful in helping to maintain unit self-sufficiency. A year ago Collegiate's math teacher went to the headmaster to ask that the school buy a small IBM computer for use by his advanced students. The headmaster did not think that a computer should go on the school budget as a normal classroom supply, but did like the idea enough to suggest that the teacher propose the purchase to a group of interested parents. The teacher did this, the parents were interested, and the math students now have a computer.

Teachers will often take the gift route without even talking to the headmaster. The woman who teaches Collegiate's first-grade Montessori class needed some new materials and suggested to some parents that they could purchase the supplies for the school and the gift would be tax-deductible. The Montessori class soon had new materials and the headmaster hadn't done a thing.

98

I still contend, however, that gifts are not a dependable way to do business, and Collegiate has never relied on them as a means of controlling operating costs. There are two other principal ways a business can keep expenses under control, and Collegiate has made good use of both.

The first of these is to minimize initial costs, actually to cut the cost of a project or activity to the lowest possible point. Minimizing costs can, of course, be achieved by using inferior materials or labor. At Collegiate our goal has been to provide superior material and faculty labor for the lowest possible price. When Collegiate's lower-school classrooms were built, for example, we had carpeting put on all the floors. It was quieter, cheaper, and easier to maintain than a tile floor. Similarly, mothers or college students drive Collegiate buses because they are cheaper than union bus drivers, and their driving "quality" is just as high. This is cost-cutting in the most direct and simple manner.

The second way Collegiate has controlled costs, and the area where the most innovating has been done, has been to make maximum use of the school's resources. This approach may not reduce the initial costs, but it can go a long way to keeping down subsequent overhead expenses.

The real secret to cost control is to get maximum production out of what you have. A business that can run around the clock is going to have a more efficient, economical operation over the long run than a company that stays open for only eight hours. We reluctantly conceded that Collegiate could not stay open all night, but we have developed some other ideas that are almost as economical. We got more production out of the teachers by switching to a trimester schedule. Also, some faculty members work for the school year-round, and in the summer they help landscape, paint, and do repair work, as well as teach summer school.

One of the great ways I believe education costs will be reduced in the future is by using older students to teach the younger ones. Volunteers from upper school provide extra help to lower-school students and tutor students from other schools who come seeking special help. Collegiate splits any fee with the student-tutor and saves itself the cost of hiring an adult tutor.

Then there is the case of the school's swimming pool. Collegiate would have been reluctant to build a pool strictly for its own use as part of the physical education program, or even as an optional activity for students. So, we arranged with the Wichita Swim Club, which did not have a pool of its own, to help build an Olympic-size swimming pool on the Collegiate campus. Our students use the pool during the day and the Swim Club practices evenings, its members paying a fee to cover the overhead while they are using it. We needed them, they needed us, and everybody's happy.

Another example of how facilities can be put to maximum use concerns Collegiate's gymnasium. The gym teacher has a gymnastics club of his own which meets evenings in Collegiate's gymnasium. In return for use of the school's gym, he teaches all the lower-school physical education classes at a reduced salary—a "loss" he makes up with income from his private evening courses. Collegiate reduces a salary cost by permitting the instructor to use a facility which would otherwise be vacant.

These are all cases where everyone benefits in some way. Nobody is being asked to surrender any time or money for the "greater good" of Collegiate School. This is cost control at its very best. Collegiate is able to reduce its budget without damaging the education product.

Salaries

In the matter of salaries, which comprise 80 percent of Collegiate's total budget, there was no question as to what method of cost control to use. It was impossible to sacrifice quality by hiring cheap—or even cheaper—labor.

If Collegiate wanted to attract and retain customers, its faculty, especially, had to be better than any local school. Cost control in faculty salaries had to be strictly a case of obtaining maximum production from the best teachers that could be found. Our philosophy and practice was to hire fewer people for higher wages to do more work.

This was a sound policy, based on business experience. A few years ago our company was prevented by a brick-layers' strike from starting construction on a factory extension. When it appeared the strike would last a while, we hired nonunion builders and paid them a dollar an hour more than the union people were asking. The job was completed in half the time the union contractor had originally estimated and the net construction cost was less, despite the higher hourly rate. The same principle was applied at Collegiate School. Our first question was always, "How can this service be performed at a lower overall cost?"

Although the main inspiration for this economizing was budgetary necessity, we found that many of our salary-cutting solutions made good sense. For example, couldn't scholarship students clean up classrooms each day or help tutor younger children and save the school the expense of hiring more help? If mothers were willing to drive a school bus to help pay for their child's tuition, why hire full-time bus drivers? Why shouldn't the headmaster do all the administrative work instead of paying a couple of bureaucrats to do it?

There is no magic formula for cutting costs, and salaries are the most difficult cost for a school to control. The educational structure forces the school to have at least one full-time teacher for every grade or course of study. There are very, very few ways a school can cut salaries and hire a full complement of teachers without undermining the education product.

Collegiate aimed to resolve this dilemma by reaching a point where each economic unit within the school was earning its maximum income. A teacher is paid the same for teaching five students as for twenty, and it was incumbent on all teachers—if they wanted to continue at Collegiate—to help the school maintain full enrollment in their courses or grades.

But, we also applied our fewer people, higher wages, more work philosophy to the faculty. This took some innovating. For instance, before Collegiate switched over to the trimester plan, it had more teachers in the upper school than the budget would support. The school faced the choice of cutting teacher salaries, or raising the tuition, or recruiting more students, or coming up with a new alternative. Collegiate did add students in time, but its first, immediate step was to devise the trimester plan. This eliminated two full-time teaching positions, actually allowed the school to raise some salaries and to keep the tuition where it was.

The teachers realized the challenge the school faced in

becoming financially self-sufficient, and they helped the innovations to be successful. It is true that under the trimester schedule the teachers had to work harder and teach a more intensive program over the full school year. But they also had fewer classes in a given day—freeing them to prepare more effective presentations for the classes —and many were paid more for an increased student load.

There is a tremendous inflationary element in the teaching profession because of the way tax-supported schools operate, and independent schools can suffer from emulation if they are not careful. In our dominant education model, teachers are secure in their jobs once they reach tenure and become locked into an escalating salary schedule set by a board of education sitting in an office millions of miles from the classroom. Neither tenure nor the salary increases have any practical relationship with a specific teacher's ability. Terrible teachers are paid exactly the same as good ones. There is too little incentive for a teacher to excel, too little accountability for a poor performance, and too little feeling of responsibility toward parents or students.

Tenure rules and salary schedules can cripple an independent school, and even the adoption of the psychology behind them can do great damage. Collegiate School had the independence, flexibility and desire to break the tenure-schedule cycle. The headmaster hires teachers he thinks can produce, and rehires those who do. Good teachers are retained, poor ones are dismissed. And the headmaster realizes that a good teacher can go "sour," just as surely as a poor instructor can improve.

As for pay, there is no salary standard at Collegiate other than the value each teacher has to the school and to its customers. This value is determined by the parents, students, other teachers and, most of all, by the headmaster, the man who has to negotiate salaries and be responsible for full enrollment. The headmaster has to act very carefully and very fairly in his negotiations with the teachers. If he should happen to lose a good, popular teacher because of a difference over salary, he is going to have to do a lot of explaining to some mighty unhappy parents and students.

This has not happened at Collegiate—yet. The headmaster does not negotiate by quoting the teacher a salary figure he thinks is right, and saying, "Take it or leave it." If he absolutely cannot grant everything a teacher requests, the headmaster will have to bargain and compromise, not walk out of the room. Both parties approach the negotiations as a business transaction. Collegiate wants good teachers to keep on teaching, build a following, develop a reputation for excellence, and produce top-notch students. These achievements will help the teacher negotiate a higher salary, to be sure, but they also benefit the entire school.

On the other hand, the headmaster will not automatically raise a teacher's salary every year or two. There is no natural law that says an employee has to get better in his job year after year and that his salary should go nowhere but up. In fact, in business I have found that the majority of people reach their maximum level of job proficiency after about five years. Are teachers any different? Why shouldn't their salaries level off after four, five, or six years if their productivity also levels off?

These are questions which *someone* has to answer, and be held accountable for, and at Collegiate the final judgment is made by the headmaster. These decisions are not always automatic: two teachers may have similar classroom situations, but deserve different salaries; and the one who has been teaching fewer years may earn the higher income. Tenure means little in and of itself. Ability, proficiency, and market demand mean a great deal. The headmaster must decide.

Some of our teachers have taken a look at the economics of their unit and said to the headmaster, "Well, here I have twenty youngsters in my class, and with each one paying $1,000 in tuition that amounts to $20,000 in income for the school. So, how come I'm only getting $10,000 [or $11,000 or $9,000] and not a bigger share of the income my 'business' takes in?"

The headmaster will then produce a cost-study breakdown of the school's total overhead which shows what general expenses each classroom incurs over a year's time in utilities, maintenance, administrative salaries, and all the other items a teacher never thinks about until confronted with the figures. Second, the headmaster will say something to the effect, "Whatever your classroom overhead, I don't think you're worth more than $10,000 [or whatever] to us at this time. Maybe next year, but not now." There is still room for them to bargain and the teacher has every opportunity to show the headmaster where he's wrong.

A few of our teachers have entertained the idea that they could start a school of their own, charge whatever tuition they wanted, and make a higher salary. And we have said, "Great, Collegiate needs the competition." None of them has actually done this as yet, but I know it can be done and hope that someone will do it.

Not long ago two public school teachers in Denver quit their jobs, rented two rooms at the local YMCA, and went into business for themselves. One taught math and science and the other English and history, for seventh- and eighth-graders. They charged $1,000 annual tuition, enrolled forty students and, by keeping the overhead down, made almost $20,000 a year apiece.

With a proliferation of independent schools a true market in the teaching profession would develop and salaries would be based exclusively on merit and productivity. Once tenure, salary schedules, and certification requirements were out of the way, the very best people would be attracted to teaching. Until then, Collegiate and other schools concerned with budget efficiency will have to fight a rearguard action against wasteful, inflated salaries.

Tuition

A business that relies on income to cover costs has to make it as easy as possible for the customer to pay. At Collegiate this has been done by setting the tuition price for the coming school year early enough to give parents time to plan the expense in the family budget. Then the school sticks to this figure.

In preparing the annual school-year budget, an educational institution faces a predicament faced by very few businesses. Teachers must be signed up early in the spring, and the salaries agreed on then will represent over three-quarters of the next school year's budget. However, at the time salaries are negotiated there is no way of knowing with absolute certainty how many students will be enrolled the following fall, or how much income the business will generate.

Parents know they can always send their children to public school for "free" and their tendency is to wait until the last minute to enroll them. To overcome this inclination, Collegiate's headmaster had to learn to make accurate projections of student enrollment and devise more reliable means of enrolling students early. Still the Board of Trustees had to live with deficits until they were offset with future income. The board's alternative was to charge Collegiate parents an extra assessment, an approach we avoided for very practical reasons. There was no way the Board of Trustees could force a parent to pay more once we agreed to a tuition rate. If we tried, the parents could just pack up and leave.

We had many prospective parents express the fear that, once they decided to enroll their children in Collegiate, there might be an additional assessment. The only way to allay this fear was for us to make sure it never happened *once*. This was a very important reassurance to give parents, the majority of whom had never before paid directly for education. They did not know what "shopping" for an education was all about and we did not want to make it any more difficult for parents to accept Collegiate and full-cost pricing than we knew it already was. If the school had ever readjusted the tuition in midyear, it would have given prospective parents a handy reason not to return.

In a market transaction it is very easy for the money involved—in this case tuition—to become a convenient customer whipping-boy. To avoid this Collegiate extended every consideration to the parent. We set the tuition early, did not alter the figure, increased tuition little from year to year, and worked to improve the academic operation to the point where the customer felt he was getting his money's worth in services. Then the trustees and headmaster used every method of gentle persuasion available to get parents to re-enroll their children well ahead of the school year.

As the quality of the school grew, parents did become more loyal and less prone to sign up their youngsters at the last minute. What really put the tuition-budget problem out of the way was the new recruiting method instituted in 1971, with the teachers themselves re-enrolling students in face-to-face talks with parents. In the first year of the new approach, the school had almost 85 percent re-enrollment and, most important, the commitments were made in the spring, at the time the budget for the coming school year was being prepared. The direct appeal by the teachers made the parents feel better about paying tuition, and having the commitments in hand early made the headmaster's budgeting job a lot easier.

Taxes and Exemptions

One of the first assignments a new organization gives its lawyers these days is to have them investigate what tax "breaks" it might get from the Internal Revenue Service. Collegiate School was no different. Since the beginning, the IRS has classified Collegiate as an eleemosynary, or charitable, institution, meaning that gifts to it can be deducted from the donor's taxable income. Second, Collegiate is exempt from property taxes, as are all schools.

I, personally, have never felt the least bit guilty about having the school accept this "favor" from the government. It has not endangered Collegiate's independence and if the school were paying property taxes we would only be financing the local public school competition. We would not lobby and play politics to get a special tax dispensation from any political body, but as long as a tax exemption is in the law, and all the school has to do is say, "We are this," then it will be used.

At the same time, the trustees and headmaster realize that the government views Collegiate's tax exemptions as a form of subsidy, and this could cause problems. The government long ago stopped using taxes exclusively for purposes of income production, and now uses them for control purposes also. The state's assumption appears to be that it owns everyone's income, and allows the people to keep a portion of it. This is seen by the government as a subsidy to every tax-paying individual and institution, and recent government history demonstrates that subsidy is a means to regulation. The government could, then, come to Collegiate School and say, "You are receiving this subsidy from us and you must, therefore, submit to our regulations. Sorry, but those are the rules of the game." And this would probably mean that Collegiate, to go on receiving its tax exemption would have to be accredited by the state Board of Education and employ only certified teachers.

It will not be too long before the federal government assumes total financial responsibility for all the nation's education costs. At that time, Washington will also have to establish national standards for school accreditation and these regulations will apply to all private and parochial schools, as well as the public system. The federal government would not tolerate the flexibility in this area that Kansas does.

When this does happen, Collegiate School will become —if it has not already—a full-fledged, tax-paying, private corporation which happens to be engaged in the business of education. We are preparing for and working toward that eventuality. There is no telling what the government will do then. At least Collegiate will be in a stronger position to resist coercion than if it were still relying on tax exemptions.

A nonpublic school that has any hope of maintaining its independence in the foreseeable future *must* have financial self-sufficiency as one of its major goals. That is the best protection against government regulation that there is.

Operations, or
Practicing the Preaching

COLLEGIATE SCHOOL'S operations reflect the philosophy of offering the best education at the lowest cost. The money spent does not come from anonymous outside sources. It is our own. The children attending the school are not the offspring of faceless parents. They are our own. We want our children to learn as much as they can while spending as little of our money as necessary. This does not require cutting corners; it requires the creation of fewer corners to be cut. If an operation was not absolutely essential, but a lot of parents wanted it nonetheless (such as sports), the headmaster said Collegiate would have the program if the parents of student-participants would agree to support it. If the parents did not do this, the plan was dropped. If an operation was essential to the school, but could not be self-supporting (such as construction), it was financed by the trustees as a capital investment. Throughout the school's history, in every operation, the working philosophy has been the same: maximum benefit for minimum cost.

Construction and Design

Collegiate School's original home was a one-story frame building with only five thousand square feet of floor space and very little land. By the end of our first year in business we were already envisioning Collegiate's growth and had drawn up a long-range plan projecting an ultimate enrollment of five hundred students in kindergarten through grade twelve. To accomplish this, we knew that more land and a better facility were essential.

We sold the building, bought some country land east of the city, and hired an architect. Our instructions to the architect were simple: design a building with the most space at the least cost and requiring as little maintenance as possible. We wanted something pleasing and useful, with no frills.

The high cost of construction (even in 1962) dictated that the money for the school building had to come from capital contributions. Most of our parents could not afford an assessment for the construction costs and we didn't want to lose any customers by trying it. Neither did the trustees have money to burn, and we carefully watched over every step of the design planning to make sure there was no waste. In an economic sense, this was "our" building, and our demands on the architect and the builders were the same as a businessman would apply in the construction of a new factory.

What resulted was a one-story, flat-roofed, brick-and-timber building that looks as though it grew naturally out of its setting on the flat Kansas prairie. The built-up roof is covered with white marble to reflect the sun and extends over the sides of the building to provide eaves large enough to protect the exterior from weather damage.

The brick-and-wood construction has reduced the school's interior maintenance to the virtual zero point. The buff bricks require no cleaning and the natural wood inside has never had to be restained (the outside wood was restained after eight years). The remaining wall space can be covered with one gallon of paint.

The interior layout is elementary, with two wings spreading out from a center section containing the offices and bathrooms. Classrooms open onto long corridors from both sides of each wing. There is little window space in the classrooms, because windows are a big construction and maintenance expense and distract students' attention.

The major design and construction innovation at Collegiate concerned floor covering. The architect assumed we wanted durable vinyl tile in the halls and classrooms, just like any other new school. *Everybody* said that with hundreds of kids tramping through the school day after day, you must have a vinyl floor. And since walking on vinyl tile creates noise, we would also be compelled to put acoustical tile on the ceilings.

The trustees decided to do some investigating before accepting this theory. Shortly before this time our company offices had been completely carpeted and I saw how this simple change improved morale, gave a cleaner appearance, and was quieter than hard surfaces. I was sold on carpeting and was convinced it could be used somehow in the new school building.

According to the architect's figures, the acoustical and vinyl tile together would cost about 75 cents per square foot, for an approximate total of $7 a square yard. A couple of the trustees went to a local carpet dealer and said, "We want to buy 1,500 yards of carpeting, providing you can give us a price under $7 per square yard that includes padding, installation, and a five-year guarantee." The dealer then offered us a continuous-filament nylon carpet at $6.50 per square yard, complete with pad, installation, and a ten-year guarantee.

We bought the carpeting and confounded the architect. This was just one of those things he had never thought of, and this was his business. *We* were paying the bill, however, and *we* were looking for ways to cut costs. With carpeting covering all Collegiate's floor space, noise was reduced and the need for acoustical tile eliminated. The classrooms and halls were far more attractive, the students felt more comfortable, and the carpeting was easier to keep clean than vinyl would have been. Collegiate's carpets are shampooed and scrubbed thoroughly twice a year, and show few signs of wear after eight years of rugged use. (The Wichita public school superintendent took one look at Collegiate's carpet, realized the advantages, and proposed to the Board of Education that carpets be put in some of the city schools. When the public heard about this there was almost a revolution. Why, some taxpayers didn't have any carpeting in their own homes! The proposal was tabled.)

Another construction innovation was Collegiate's use of electrical heat. The trustees reasoned that, over the years, the price of natural gas heat was going to go up, and electrical heating costs would come down from what they were then. This has proven to be correct, and in a couple of years Collegiate will be paying a lower heating bill than if it had gone with natural gas in the beginning. The local electric company, eager to demonstrate the benefits of their product to the community, gave us a discount on the installation costs.

Installing electrical heat had several fringe advantages. We did not have to put flues up through the roof, saving on construction costs and preserving the clean, linear design. Also, electric heat removed the danger of fire from combustible gas, and this fact, together with the predominantly brick construction, made the school virtually fireproof. This was an important point with parents worried about their children attending a school outside the city limits, miles from the nearest fire department.

Four years after the first construction project was completed enough grades had been added to require a separate upper-school classroom building. We handed the builder the same plan used for the lower-school structure and had him erect another exactly like the first. As everyone was pleased with the original, why not duplicate it and eliminate the architect's fee?

It could be argued that today's increased material and labor costs prohibit parents from constructing facilities like those at Collegiate. I am not sure what these facilities would cost at today's prices, or what sort of structure could be had for the $150,000 which our first building cost. The important point, however, is that by using a simple design, efficient construction, and materials requiring little maintenance, anyone can have a school building that will be low-cost in the long run.

An example of how the construction picture can change to the advantage of a school is Collegiate's swimming pool. There was no way we could have afforded to build an enclosed pool at the time we were constructing classrooms. The expense was prohibitive. By the time some Collegiate parents did start thinking about putting in a pool, a man in northern Kansas had invented a nylon bubble enclosure supported by air pressure produced by a fan. We saw a demonstration and were convinced the idea would work as a swimming pool dome. The bubble keeps the pool area heated in the winter, it can be removed during the warm months, and it costs a fraction of what it would have been to put up a permanent pool building.

Collegiate was the first school in Kansas with a bubble building, wall-to-wall carpeting, and an electrical heating system. People in the community couldn't believe what Collegiate was doing; these were all very "radical" ideas to them. The school could afford to pay no attention. No one at Collegiate was running for public office. We were free to look for the most economical, efficient construction and design available, radical or not.

Scholarships

In the very early days of Collegiate School the Board of Trustees decided that at least 10 percent of each year's tuition income would be set aside for scholarship assistance. We did not want to deny use of the educational facilities to a qualified, eager child whose parents could not, or would not, pay the tuition.

This scholarship fund is available annually for the headmaster to dispense as he sees fit. The trustees have nothing to do with its administration. The headmaster knows the applicants and their parents better than anyone and, as chief operating officer, he must live with the decision concerning who gets the scholarship aid and how much.

The way Collegiate's headmaster has preferred to allocate the scholarship money is, for example, to give twenty students partial help, rather than hand five children a totally free ride. By giving only partial aid the school is able to help more students and also to have reluctant parents become accustomed to paying directly for at least a portion of their children's education.

Frequently parents of a scholarship student have found the family economic situation improved and, by then, are convinced that a good education is worth paying for. They assume full payment for their child's schooling. In some instances parents who could afford the whole tuition have refused to pay a cent, even though the child wanted to attend Collegiate. Students in this situation have received complete scholarships, and most of the parents, seeing their child suddenly enjoying school and learning, then agreed to pay the child's full tuition.

A school that practices full-cost pricing cannot underwrite too many students or it will go broke. Yet, a scholarship fund is essential in attracting the qualified student and the interested parent, who could not otherwise enroll, as they will help build the school's reputation. Collegiate needed customers in order to produce the happy parents and successful students who were later to become the school's most effective "salesmen." The scholarship fund helped attract those customers.

In return for scholarship assistance, Collegiate asks the student—in some cases the parents—to do some form of work for the school. This lowers maintenance costs and, more important, allows the student actually to pay his own way. The child is not intimidated by the fact that he is receiving "something for nothing," and no other student can say to him, "My parents are subsidizing you." Collegiate students know "there ain't no such thing as a free education."

Scholarship students clean up Collegiate's classrooms every day after school, saving the expense of another janitor. The students usually take one classroom apiece, straighten the chairs, wash the blackboards, sweep the room, and are done in ten or fifteen minutes. Others prefer to come out to the school on weekends or summer days, and help with the landscaping, gardening, and other outside maintenance. When the student is too young for this sort of work, one or both of the parents contribute their time and labor. Mothers work in the library, drive buses and tutor, or the fathers will contribute skills in carpentry, wiring, painting, and other types of repair work. Somebody does something, and nobody gets a free ride.

Libraries and Librarians

A few years ago one of Collegiate's parents donated the money for construction of a library wing onto the upper school. The addition was built, books were bought and donated, and a librarian hired.

Today I am convinced that a library per se with no other use is unnecessary in any elementary or secondary school. This was one of those gifts that the trustees might have looked at more closely. Although Collegiate needed the space it didn't really need the thousands of books, a librarian, and all the extra overhead costs. Two years after our library was built the headmaster released the librarian, eliminating an extra annual salary. The duties that were formerly performed by a "professional" librarian are now shared by mothers of children on scholarship and by older students who volunteer their time.

A library is a luxury that should not be indulged in unless the school has so much money it doesn't know what to do with it. Even then a more beneficial use of the funds can be found. There is a romantic attachment most educationists place on libraries that is not supported by experience and facts. Most students will not use the library except as a place to study, a function that can be fulfilled by an empty classroom if one is available. The students should have enough material in their course textbooks and other reading provided by the teacher to eliminate the time or need for library books.

Collegiate teachers all play the role of librarians, as any good instructor should. Their students are kept busy and up with the curriculum through assigned reading. The books necessary for a course are provided by the school on the teachers' recommendations. If a student should have the time and desire to seek outside reading, the teacher can usually either provide the book from his or her own library or can locate a copy on short notice.

When students are busy and the teachers are fully in control of the course and the class, what does the school need with an expensive library? Sure, I know Collegiate already has one, a very attractive, comfortable room, that is constantly used by students, faculty, and parents for a variety of purposes. The best I can say is that as a library exclusively it would not receive enough use to justify its cost. Fortunately, the donor of our library allowed the building to be designed in such a manner as to accommodate almost any use.

Lunch

When Collegiate put up its lower-school building, it faced the problem of how and where it should feed its students at noontime. Some students brought their lunch, the school had to provide for the rest. It was economically unfeasible to build a separate cafeteria. Collegiate's budget did not contain funds for cafeteria help and equipment, and the school could not afford to have the cafeteria space standing idle except for an hour or two each day. Collegiate is in the education business, not the food business.

One of the trustees suggested that we put the lunch operation up for bids. It was a very normal business proposition and it was accepted. The headmaster calculated the maximum number of meals needed during a coming school year and the trustees asked caterers, restaurant owners, and cafeteria operators how much they would charge to provide these meals. There was a lot of bidding on the proposal and the contract was finally awarded to a fellow who ran a cafeteria. He did such a competent job that Collegiate has renewed his contract every year. In the meantime, he has signed up other businesses as lunch-time customers, sold his cafeteria, and become a full-time caterer.

The caterer prepares the food each day in his central kitchen, trucks it to the school, provides the serving help, and cleans up afterward. Collegiate divides the cost of the meals among the students who eat at the school, with the charge scaled according to age groups, and adds a percentage of the utilities overhead to cover the heat and power costs incurred while the assembly room is being used as a cafeteria. Only the parents of students who want to eat lunch and sign up for it are charged. If a child forgets to bring his lunch one day, he can eat at the school for $1.

The school does not imitate those universities which require all students to pay room and board, and then try to save money by lowering food quality. Everyone has to buy the service, so the university knows the students can't do anything about food except not eat in the school cafeteria—which ends up as another saving for the school.

Collegiate isn't trying to make money on its food operation. It demands quality food and sets a price that will cover the costs. If you're going to perform a service and not charge what it costs, you'll have problems. Collegiate doesn't need any problems. The students eat well, the caterer is satisfied with his contract, and the school has avoided another potential headache and can concentrate on education with one less distraction.

Transportation

Collegiate has no choice but to be in the busing business, if it wants customers. The business has to pay for itself, however, and parents who want their children to ride the buses are charged an annual rate. Their payments buy the vehicles and finance their maintenance. An interesting sidelight to this arrangement was the revelation that parents who don't want to bother with driving their kids to school will pay anything for transportation. The same parents who complain about tuition will pay for transportation without question. No price is too high to save some mothers and fathers the trouble of getting up and dressed early enough to drive into school.

Collegiate owns two fourteen-passenger Chevrolet vanbuses, and each was paid for with income from the transportation charge. In 1971 the school had to buy its own seventy-passenger bus on short notice (previously it had been leased) and this, too, will pay for itself within three years.

There are no bus drivers' salaries on Collegiate's budget. The driving is done by mothers of scholarship students and, in one case, by a local college student who volunteered his services in return for having the van-bus to use for his own transportation to and from the university.

Athletics

Every small city, town, and village in America is crazy about its local high school athletic teams. The Board of Education can cut any item in the school's budget except that for interschool athletics. If it cuts in that tender spot, the community will have the board members tarred and feathered. The people want winning teams!

I think this is totally wrong. Team sports have nothing to do with formal education. It is fine for a school to have football, basketball, and baseball teams competing with other schools as long as the programs are financed by the parents of the students participating. If the parents don't want to pay—no team.

This is the way Collegiate handles the athletics operation. When a boy wants to play on the football team, his parents pay a $30 fee. The money is used for the coach's salary, new equipment, referee's fees, and other items in the football budget. The same goes for Collegiate's basketball, field hockey, track, and tennis operations. (It does not apply to the school's physical education program, which is made available to all students and is covered by tuition.) Actually, as of 1971, the athletic operation at

Collegiate was not yet completely self-supporting. The school was still assuming a small part of the cost. This situation will be corrected as the school increases the game admission charges and uses this income to offset deficits.

Otherwise, athletics have not been a part of the general education budget. The swimming pool and gymnasium were built by fathers interested in seeing Collegiate develop competitive teams. The tiers of spectators' bleachers in the gym were installed after the trustees came up with a new "rule" following a close basketball game: "The father of a boy who scores the winning basket for Collegiate in the last few seconds of a game has to buy the next set of bleachers." The baseball diamonds were laid out by the Wichita YMCA, which uses them for its own programs on spring and summer evenings.

The parents and students at Collegiate are as proud of their athletic teams as the citizens of any community, and they support them with the fan's fanaticism. At the same time, the parents understand that athletics do not belong in the education budget. The parents who really want team sports will support the program and let the school get on with education.

Public Relations

The best public relations department an independent school can have consists of happy, enthusiastic parents and successful students. People will notice the students, listen to the parents, and start talking about the school.

Talk about Collegiate School began as community members started to realize that our parents had enrolled their children voluntarily because they wanted the youngsters to have the best education available. The parents did not seek out Collegiate for political reasons or for any "snob appeal" it might have. In fact they were eager to have others come and share the experience. The parents' enthusiasm for Collegiate's academics tended to disarm skeptics and start them thinking about educational alternatives in an objective light. The outstanding performance of the students, at Collegiate and in college, attested to the school's academic quality and created more talk.

Collegiate considered many approaches to the public relations problem before deciding to do nothing formally. We experimented with promotional breakfasts, open houses, expensive mailing brochures, and even discussed hiring an advertising agency. None of the strategies we considered or actually tried proved helpful. Even the newspaper ads in the school's early days were discontinued when they attracted so few customers.

Some Collegiate programs do serve to create good public relations. These are programs which bring "outside" youngsters out to Collegiate. They include the Swim Club using the pool; the YMCA playing on the baseball diamonds; public school students being tutored, taking summer school courses, and attending interschool athletic events at Collegiate. Otherwise, Collegiate's public relations operation is mostly by word of mouth.

Statistics

Statistics are the steady diet of bureaucrats. Bureaucracies take root and grow when demand for statistics increases—a demand by the bureaucrats themselves, their bosses, and the public. In a school statistics are what board members, teachers, and parents want so they will know where the school stands, how "good" it is, how its students compare with others in the city, in the state, in the nation.

The result is that the school suddenly finds itself burdened with a staff of officials who spend a good part of their time gathering statistics, fitting them together, rearranging them, and trying to have figures make the school look good. I make the flat statement that there is not a city of any size in this country where the people will not claim that the local school system is one of the "ten best" in the country. They say this because some school official has shown them the statistics to "prove" it, and because it makes the people feel better about all the taxes they are pouring into the schools every year.

This is all meaningless. Statistics have no authority in and of themselves. There is no set of figures that can show how well motivated students are, what teachers have to offer, or how much wisdom a curriculum imparts. But parents want this authority, nevertheless. They want to be reassured that their child and his school are not "below average."

I see this same thirst for statistical authority in business, and it is just as nonsensical. If I were to boast that our company makes 99 percent of all the boxes sold in Wichita, what would that mean? Our next customer cares only about how good his boxes are. Statistics won't mean very much if a box falls apart.

Collegiate parents are normal, however, and I even find myself quoting statistics to show how well the school's students are doing on tests or how well the graduates have done in college. This would never be my first or only defense for the school, but the figures are a handy shortcut.

The difference at Collegiate is that no one makes a fetish out of statistics and no bureaucrats spend time collecting them—and no one has ever, ever said that Collegiate is one of the "ten best" of *anything* in the country. If any parents should be interested, the headmaster can show them national public and private school grade figures that come into his office and take no time to compile. The parents can also see how their children compare with the other students in their classes.

Aside from what guidance these few statistics provide, parents must make their own judgments on how well Collegiate is educating their children. If they are closely following the child's intellectual development, the parents will know the answer and no set of figures can tell them better. When parents care, statistics don't matter.

Grading

The one statistic that Collegiate does furnish parents is the child's grade. I realize there is some controversy in education circles over the value of giving students numerical or letter grades. There has never been any question about doing this at Collegiate. The parent-customers want to know how their children are doing in school and grades are one way to provide them with this information.

Collegiate has devised a unique grading system that tells parents exactly where their children stand in a class and how consistent a student's work has been. At the end of the semester the parents receive a report from each of their children's teachers. On the report the individual teacher will list all the grade scores—anywhere from 0 to 100—of every student for every test the class had during the term, and will circle those grades received by the child of the parent the report is going to.

For example, the report from the French I teacher may show four columns of nine figures, representing the four tests given during that semester and the grades received on each by the nine French I students. No names are given, only grades. The teacher will have circled one number in each column—the grades which the child in question scored on the four tests. Parents will receive a similar report from all the teachers their child had that semester.

The test-result average will constitute 75 percent of the student's final grade in each class. The remaining 25 percent is determined by the teacher on the basis of the student's daily preparation, recitations, quiz scores, and extra work (projects, outside reading, etc.). The final grades are also numerical, with anything below 70 being a failing grade.

Grades, like any other statistic, are fallible and can never be viewed as the final word on a student's performance. Only the individual student can truly know how much he gets out of a course or out of all his years in school. The best that grades can do is to provide parents and the students with a semester-to-semester progress report. This is an important consideration for them and provides all the justification Collegiate needs for its grading system.

Tutoring

Each Collegiate student receives individual attention from his teachers, and those who are falling behind in their work are helped to catch up. This is part of the teachers' job, and part of the challenge of making independent education work.

The amount of time spent tutoring students is entirely up to the teacher. When a teacher has given as much extra assistance to a student as he or she can without neglecting other duties, the student is directed to another tutorial program within the school. Collegiate provides an extra teacher in the lower grades to work with academic problems during the day. Upper-school students also help tutor the younger children, apparently believing the saying "If you want to learn, teach somebody."

Should this assistance still be insufficient, the teacher will recommend that the parents get tutorial help from outside Collegiate's program. A professional tutor from the community may be suggested, or the parents may offer to pay the teacher separately to work evenings with their child. (Many states have laws prohibiting teachers from taking money from parents to tutor their children. Admittedly, there is always a danger that a dishonest teacher can mislead and cheat parents. This has not happened at Collegiate, as I am sure it would not in any school where the teachers and parents work closely together.)

Collegiate's faculty members are hired to give students as much educational service as they can in return for a flat tuition fee. The parents understand the faculty's responsibility, they appreciate an extra effort and know when teachers have done all they can to help a student. Very few parents have complained that they were not getting as much service for their child as they had paid for. We have had many instances where parents approached a teacher voluntarily and said: "You've done enough on your own. This is a good program, we want to stay in it and we don't mind spending a little more money if it will help our youngster. Now, we'd like for you to spend another hour a week with our child. How much do you charge?"

Collegiate's tutorial operation has been so successful with its own students that in 1970 the school started a program to assist public school students. Immediately after the first marking period in the Wichita public schools an ad was placed in the local newspaper inviting students with academic problems to come to Collegiate afternoons or evenings and be tutored. Many youngsters responded and several of them, once exposed to Collegiate, talked their parents into letting them become full-time students at the school.

This tutorial program proved to be a gold mine for some of Collegiate's brighter upper-school students. They tutored the public school youngsters and split the fee with the school. A good tutor could work with two students at a time—putting one on a teaching machine and working individually with the other, then switching—and by doing this two or three times a week could earn up to $50 a month.

This is a program which I hope Collegiate will continue. The school has the facilities, equipment, machines, and manpower available to do the job. It's like a business that achieves maximum production only when it runs three shifts, twenty-four hours a day. Every business should try to get the most production out of its facilities.

Schedules, Hours and Assorted Impedimenta

When Collegiate School began to grow rapidly, and some classes increased from five to ten and then to fifteen students, a lot of parents said to the headmaster, "Oh, you're going to crowd the classes; why do you want to do that?" Then they would be quiet for the rest of the year when they saw that their children were still getting a good education.

The same happened when Collegiate switched from two semesters a year to the trimester plan. Parents were convinced we were going straight to hell. "You're sacrificing a good education to save a little money," they'd say. "Are you ready to pay more?" the headmaster would ask. When these folks saw that the quality of education had in fact been improved by the new schedule, they were satisfied.

Most people, whatever they say to the contrary, are afraid of change. The men who work in our factory don't ever want anything to change except their pay. People don't want anyone to disturb their routine. Parents of school children are no different.

Collegiate School had to change, however. The school labored under no compulsion other than to provide a quality education, pay its own way, and survive in what marketplace existed. The headmaster or trustees did not have to please every taxpayer group in the city, or bow to the wishes of bureaucrats in the state capital. Collegiate wanted only to be good, and to achieve that status required experimentation. The plan was to change gradually and bring the school's customers along gently.

The main focus of Collegiate's changes was education structure. This included such items as scheduling, academic requirements, length of classes, length of the school week and year and, to a much lesser extent, class size (which we were determined to hold to twenty students in all but the most exceptional cases). All the structural factors that Collegiate had to contend with are part of the education "tradition" in America. Collegiate inherited these trappings and then had to figure out ways to do away with them. We found that structural restrictions do more to impede learning than to help it, and this was not our intention.

The decision to implement the trimester schedule is probably the most "radical" change Collegiate has made. We had started out like any other school, with students in the upper school taking five subjects each semester, five classes a day, five days a week. Out of curiosity I asked the headmaster one day, "Do you really think that you can lecture five days a week in one course, an hour each day and be effective?" And he replied, "Heck, no, no teacher can." To which I said, "Then let's try something different."

Today Collegiate offers three 12-week semesters per year, instead of the previous two 18-week terms. During each semester the faculty teaches each subject only three times a week, with classes lasting about eighty-five minutes. The brighter students can take four courses each semester, earning twelve credits a year where they received only ten before. The slower learners are advised to take three courses some semesters or a combination totaling ten credits for the year.

The results of this change have been outstanding. Fewer teachers can teach more material during each semester and have more time to prepare for doing it. A bright student can complete his college entrance requirements by the end of his junior year, and spend his senior year taking electives, serving as a teacher's aide, or attending classes at a local university (for which Collegiate pays his tuition).

No bureaucratic approval was needed for Collegiate to make this change. The Board of Trustees said, "Go ahead" and it was done. The parents who objected at first all love it now.

The matter of when a student should leave school is another structural area where the traditional method doesn't make sense. If a child can do the work and take all the basic courses by the time he is fifteen or sixteen, and is ready for college, he should be able to go if he wants to. Likewise, a child should not feel like a fool if he chooses to stay in school for a year or two after the rest of his class graduates. I've seen a lot of Collegiate students who were not emotionally and academically ready for college, even though they had completed the required courses. Another year at Collegiate would have been a great help. But they had finished twelve years, so away they went.

The sooner we can break away from the idea that college preparedness equals twelve grades and x-number of courses completed, the better off education will be. Why should a person go on to college if he hasn't learned all a school has to offer? No reason—social convention says he should. Collegiate is trying to break the mold by encouraging students to stay an extra year and take courses they might have missed, or brush up on weak subjects. It has not been easy.

Independent schools have the flexibility to make changes when they think they will benefit the education product, and to explain these decisions directly to the customers. When we instituted by-invitation classes, open only to students whom the teacher wanted in the class, the headmaster received bitter complaints from parents of students who were not invited: "How come this boy over here is getting this course and mine isn't, when I'm paying the same tuition?" The headmaster explains: "Because this boy over here works harder. Get your child to do more work and use his abilities and he might make the class."

By the same token, when parents of bright youngsters complain that the teachers are spending too much time with slow learners, the headmaster points out that Collegiate's flexibility allows the teachers to work with students as individuals, not as a mass where the teaching is pegged to one level. Collegiate can offer two or three different learning tracks and not have to worry about public reaction. A child may be placed in a slow English class and the most difficult math class, depending on his abilities. This is merely putting independence to work for the benefit of everyone.

There are still many areas where Collegiate has yet to make needed changes. What is the reason for holding classes a certain number of days per year, or for closing schools down three months every year? In the old days schools closed in the summer so the farm children could help their fathers, a consideration that doesn't apply in many areas today.

Collegiate is working toward the day when the school can be open all year around, with four semesters offered during the year and a two-week break between each term. A student could then attend school as many semesters a year as he wanted, taking one, two, or even three terms off if he wanted to work or travel or do something else. This would be a giant step toward a true market in education. Both parent and student would shop around for precisely the academic products that they wanted, at the time and place of their choice.

10

Customer Relations, or
The Care and Feeding of
the Education Consumer

THE CLOSER THE operating personnel of a business are to the customers, the better the chances of success for the business. When the producer and consumer are operating in close quarters, there is little lag between the time the customer first feels a service need and the time the appropriate operating officer knows of it and responds. This is customer relations at its best.

The situation should be the same at an independent school, where parents and students fulfill the role of consumers in an education marketplace. The headmaster and faculty must have the primary responsibility for recruiting customers, satisfying their needs, and maintaining their patronage. At the same time the chief executive officer must realize that the customer is not "always right" and that it is impossible for a business to satisfy every customer's every desire.

The potential conflict between desire and ability-to-provide has not arisen at Collegiate School. The operating personnel and the customer are—except for isolated cases on both sides—equally dedicated to the goal of quality education. Both producer and consumer enter the relationship voluntarily and are aware of the responsibilities this freedom entails. By treating parents and students as customers whose patronage the school wants, good customer relations have come naturally.

Recruiting

We have found that the best way to recruit new customers for Collegiate is to have enthusiastic parents talking about the school, and children at Collegiate performing well and setting a good example. Members of the community hear these people talking and see how much the children are learning. They become interested in Collegiate and decide to have a talk with the headmaster. Collegiate has no organized drive to recruit new customers. If a friend expresses interest in Collegiate, our parents are advised not to become personally involved. They are urged to tell their friends how to apply, and leave it at that.

We started off doing just the opposite and got our fingers burned. When the school was new and had to enlarge its enrollment quickly to survive, we grew frustrated because other parents—many of whom we knew shared our feelings about education—did not come running. We resorted to recruiting overkill. The trustees, headmaster, teachers, and active parents pursued potential customers directly, wherever they could be found. We made our argument and then, if there was the slightest twinkle of interest, we virtually dragged the listener out to Collegiate. We got a few good students, several bad ones, and created a lot of animosity.

The best customer a business can have is the one who offers his patronage of his own free will. In those early days we forgot this market principle. The main thing our proselytizing did was to create new hostility to Collegiate and to intensify hostility that already existed. I suspect that an independent school in any area where there has been none before is going to serve as a lightning rod for public hostility. The people behind the venture must be prepared for this. It will happen whenever people practice what they believe. This does not make recruiting new customers any easier, but it helps if the school's promoters are not out stirring the pot—at least not in the beginning.

The most interesting reaction from the people I talked to was that a lot of friends and associates who had previously been sharing my dissatisfaction with public education were suddenly that system's biggest defenders when I began boosting Collegiate. "Public schools are good enough for our kids," the common refrain went, "why aren't they good enough for yours?" I had the distinct impression that the establishment of Collegiate represented a direct challenge to them, and that it was not a challenge taken lightly.

Among those most hostile to our independent education venture were my supposed allies in the John Birch Society. For all their talk about Big Government and "subversion" in the classroom, these defenders of liberty kept their children in the public schools and criticized Collegiate. They preferred to write nasty letters-to-the-editor about the local "little Red schoolhouse" than actually to make a commitment to build a better school. They sounded no different on the subject of Collegiate from liberals, Democrats, and Republicans I talked with. Politics, I've learned, has little to do with principle.

This attitude on the part of my fellow Birch Society members did not prevent the more "moderate" members of the community from accusing Collegiate of being some sort of "right-wing" school, with a curriculum heavily laden with the gospel according to Goldwater. Hostility toward Collegiate was strictly bipartisan.

Not all community reaction to Collegiate was negative, of course, but even when parents did express genuine interest, we ran the risk of making enemies. The trustees, headmaster, and teachers all had the experience of persuading a friend to apply and then finding that the friend's child was not qualified or could not do the work once admitted. And the parents would blame whichever one of us got them into the situation for the school's action toward the child. Our people would be so thrilled that their friends were applying to Collegiate, only to discover later that they had made an enemy for life.

The alternative, we learned, was to boost the school and then leave the decision to apply strictly up to the individual parents. "Go ahead and sell the school to your friends," the parents are told today, "and if they seem interested send them to see the headmaster. Keep your fingers out of it. Don't tell them they can get in and don't try to convince the headmaster they should be accepted."

Once this lesson had sunk in I was continually surprised at seeing people with whom I had casually discussed the school go to Collegiate on their own, have their children tested and admitted. I might have talked to them about Collegiate in my home, during a business meeting, or at some social activity, but not necessarily with the idea of recruiting a new customer. If I had tried to pressure them into applying, they might have been turned off Collegiate and never shown any interest.

Parents who are truly concerned with their child's education will listen to what Collegiate parents have to say. They will also look at our students and perhaps see that they are learning more than children—even their own— attending another school. This achievement will give Collegiate parents a credibility they would never have by just talking. Our school's success is due more to the reputation of its students than to any other single factor.

A second way Collegiate students have been effective "recruiting officers" is through their conversations with friends when they are playing or socializing outside of school. The non-Collegiate youngsters hear what our students are doing in school and become interested. There have been many instances where the child took the initiative and urged his parents to go to Collegiate and inquire about admission.

Once a business has a customer's patronage, it cannot assume that this will always be so. The next job is for the business to be sure it keeps the customer, and this also involves a form of recruiting. Collegiate's headmaster used to contact every parent with a child enrolled at the school and urge them to re-enroll for the next year. When they dallied, he would send a letter, make a telephone call, or have another visit.

I thought this was a very inefficient, time-consuming method of getting re-enrollments and that it did not place the burden where it ought to be. If each teacher was in charge of an individual "business" within the school, why shouldn't the teachers be responsible for attracting and keeping the customers? As an answer to my own question, I suggested to the headmaster that teachers be given the duty of visiting the parents of every student in their class and talking to them about signing up for the next school year.

The headmaster relayed the idea to the teachers, they thought about it and came up with their own version. The way it worked out was that a teacher, say the third-grade instructor, would invite "her parents" to the school one evening and have the fourth-grade teacher tell the parents what their children would be doing the next year. The same thing was done at the upper-school level, except that several teachers were present to describe the program for each course. The parents were urged to sign up that evening, and those who did not then re-enroll were visited in their homes.

This was the best treatment our customers had ever received. It was respectful and considerate. The operating personnel closest to them—the individual teachers—were seeking the customers out and requesting their continued patronage. The customers responded to the attention by giving Collegiate 85 percent on-the-spot re-enrollment.

Admissions

Admissions to Collegiate School are handled by the headmaster and a three-member faculty committee in each school. The trustees have nothing to do with who does and does not get into Collegiate. When the decision is made to apply to Collegiate, the initial step is for the child to be given achievement and I.Q. tests appropriate for his age group. The results of these tests are what the admissions people will look at first.

We decided early in Collegiate's history that to offer an above-average education the school had to recruit above-average students. This meant rejecting students with disciplinary, academic, or emotional problems. I believe there is a place in the market for a school catering to problem children, but given our goals, philosophy, and situation as the first independent school in Wichita, Collegiate could not be it.

The fact that Collegiate prefers students with an I.Q. of at least 110—or about 10 points above the national average—does not mean that its academic standards are iron-clad and inflexible. The Admissions Committee members do not judge a child only by his I.Q. A student with a 100 I.Q. who is highly motivated will most likely have a better scholastic record than a lazy student with a 125 I.Q. score.

The headmaster and faculty members on the Admissions Committee must look at the child's test scores and decide whether or not he has the intelligence horsepower to handle the Collegiate curriculum. They are all sufficiently familiar with the school's academic program to know what it demands of a student, so this decision is not arbitrary.

If a child is behind in his achievement, it is no big problem. He can most likely make up lost ground. But if the child has achieved a certain level, and his test scores indicate that he cannot reach the higher level which Collegiate might demand, then there is no way he will be able to do the work. To admit this child out of sympathy or for any nonacademic reason would be placing future grief on the child, his parents, and the school.

One reason faculty members sit on Collegiate's Admissions Committee is to guard against faulty decisions. If the members did admit a student who could positively not do the work, they would hear about it from their fellow teachers. On the other hand, when the committee approves a student who is near the line and will need some special faculty attention in helping him to do the program, the teachers on the committee will subsequently see to it that this is done.

The next step in the admissions process is an interview with the child, even those applying for kindergarten. Here the admissions people try to determine how highly motivated the child may be. There is no way to describe this judgment—the people involved have learned over the years what to look for. A child who impresses the Admissions Committee as not much caring where he goes to school, or what he learns, is refused admittance, no matter what his I.Q. If a child wants to do the work, but does not have an exceptional I.Q., the teachers will admit him and do everything they can to help.

Collegiate uses its independence to accommodate all types of students, putting each on the learning track to which the test scores indicate he belongs. Consequently, the admissions people are always looking for the highly motivated student with an I.Q. in the 100-110 range. These are the students the school can help the most and who are the most rewarding for teachers to work with.

The final admissions step is a meeting of the parents with the headmaster and Admissions Committee. By this time the decision whether or not to admit the child has usually been made, but a sour-parent interview can reverse an applicant's approval. The parent who walks in and says, "I'm glad you've taken my child, because I can't make him behave," or "I hope you can make my boy want to study," is promptly shown the door.

The purpose of the interview is for the parents to learn exactly what to expect from the school and what the school expects of them. The headmaster describes the material which the child will be studying, at what level and speed, and the reasons the particular program was selected. The parents are told of their responsibility to create a home environment where learning is stressed, and that they must become deeply involved with their child's learning if they want the most Collegiate has to offer.

Yet, as important as the parents' role is, the school does not like to disqualify a child because the Admissions Committee members dislike the parents' attitude. In fact, I would go so far as to say that Collegiate has helped some children rise above their parents. There have been students who were really working, learning, and finding themselves, while their parents were absorbed in other things—their jobs, domestic fights, alcohol, divorces—and not paying any attention to their children.

All through the admissions process the Collegiate representatives avoid the attitude (found in many private schools) that the school is doing the parents a big favor by admitting their children. They honestly want the parent and child to feel that the school is serving them as customers and that this relationship will be maintained and honored for as long as they choose to continue their patronage.

Dismissals

Dismissing a student is the hardest part of the headmaster's job. The more students that Collegiate dismisses, the more it is saying that the Admissions Committee doesn't know what it is doing. It is not easy for any business to confess ignorance in an area where it wants to excel.

Collegiate would like the public to believe that its education operation can do a great job with every student who comes there. This plainly is not the case and never will be. The school personnel have to be honest with themselves and with their customers, or else start lowering educational standards.

It especially hurts the school to have to dismiss students who just cannot keep up with the rest of their class. Collegiate's teachers are proud people who do not admit defeat easily, and it distresses them when a child must go back to the public schools, where he will receive no special help. The headmaster and teachers will do everything possible to help slow-learning students before they are dismissed: tutor and work with them until there is nothing more that can be done. There is a point, however, where the teacher must stop trying or risk neglecting the other students.

There is much less of a problem with the students who *won't* do the work, or who are dismissed for disciplinary reasons. The child who is causing trouble in class and preventing other students from learning might be dismissed at the end of the day, while the academic dismissal will be postponed until the end of the school year. A student who is disruptive and pays no attention to the education which the teacher is offering can ruin a class if not dismissed immediately. If the school avoided this action, the other students and the parents would not long tolerate the disruption. Collegiate would be offending its customers and failing in its responsibilities to them.

The teachers handle disciplinary situations up to the point where, in their opinion, dismissal of the "problem" student is the only solution. Faculty members cannot dismiss a student outright. The headmaster must make the final dismissal decision and also be the one to explain his action to the parents of the student involved. It is unfair to the parents to have one person kick their children out and then get the explanation from someone else.

These meetings with the parents are a real test of the headmaster. He must be diplomatic, honest, and try to make the separation as amiable as possible. There is no way for him to tell the parents that their child is a trouble-maker and have them like it, even if they know it is true. So, the parents get their tuition money back and the headmaster tells them as nicely as he can why the school can no longer be of any help to their child.

We have had parents of dismissed children who left Collegiate and started telling everyone they felt that the school was "no damn good." Sometimes their friends understood that their children had academic or discipline problems, sometimes they didn't. It was difficult to combat that sort of bad-mouthing until the parents lost their credibility. The school cannot go around chasing down every criticism and rumor being spread about it. Collegiate had to go ahead, do its job, build its reputation, and try to avoid making enemies.

Parents who send their children to Collegiate School have burned a lot of bridges. They sever ties with the public system and this may alienate friends, relatives, and business associates. It is a tough decision for parents to make, and the trustees, headmaster, and teachers at Collegiate respect the parents' integrity. Should the school instead turn around and treat the parents (or students) unfairly or arbitrarily, it would be guilty of cruel, irrational treatment of decent people. This must be kept in mind when teachers recommend dismissal and when the headmaster actually does dismiss a student. The parents will have to go back and "eat crow" in front of all those people to whom they have been justifying their child's attendance at Collegiate—a tougher ordeal for most parents than the decision to come to Collegiate in the first place. The school must, then, give the child every consideration before dismissing him and, when dismissal is unavoidable, handle the situation as gently as possible.

Complaints

Customers should take their complaints to the person most responsible for causing the problem. I am convinced that a business that follows this policy, instead of shuttling customers off to a vice-president in charge of complaints, will have a far more efficient operation and more loyal customers than one that does not.

The argument against this proposition is that business personnel would be overwhelmed by nagging, carping customers and could not perform their regular duties. This would be true if the business did not do good work. If one of my customers doesn't like the way a salesman handled an account and calls me about it, I tell him to talk to the salesman, not to me. If either the customer or the salesman is not satisfied with the outcome of this confrontation, only then do I—reluctantly—get involved.

It is easy to sympathize with parents who have children enrolled in schools where complaints are lodged with a vice-principal or assistant headmaster employed specifically to "take the heat." The parents seldom, if ever, get to talk to the people usually most responsible for the complaint—the teacher. Meanwhile, the bureaucrat hired to hear complaints treats his assignment like the "job" it is. His expertise is in making the parents feel listened-to, soothing the worried brow, minimizing the grievance, defending the institution—in short, doing everything but getting to the root of the problem by making the teachers accountable for their actions. The introduction of an arbitrary third force into the basic producer-consumer market relationship is bound to weaken the business structure, undermine product quality, and offend the customers.

Each teacher at Collegiate School constitutes a one-man "complaint department." The customer goes to see the individual about whom he had a complaint. If parents should first go to the headmaster, they are told to see the teacher. The headmaster becomes involved with complaints only when they cannot be resolved between parent and teacher, or when they concern general school policy. Also, parents will sometimes have a complaint that cannot be delicately presented to the teacher, such as the one mentioned earlier regarding an instructor's competence, and will go to see the headmaster.

Collegiate's bureaucracy of assistants-to and department heads was nipped in the bud several years ago. The new complaints procedure saved us administrative salaries and improved relations between the parents and teachers. The producer and consumer are brought together as closely as they can ever be, in a direct one-to-one relationship.

The result is mutual respect. Collegiate teachers are not deluged by complaining customers. Our parents pay teachers to educate their children and are close enough to the learning process to know what this job entails. They do not want anything to prevent the teacher from performing the job, and so they tend to leave the faculty alone except for specific complaints.

Discipline

Any institution that is as deeply involved in people's lives as a school is with the lives of children must eventually face up to the questions: How *far* do we get involved? How much do we interfere? To what degree do we dictate how these lives are to be lived? No matter how extraordinarily difficult a resolution of this problem may be, the school must answer its own questions honestly or suffer serious conflicts with its customers.

The place to begin is for the people who organize and establish the school to decide what type of education they want to offer to what type of student. The next decision should concern the atmosphere, or learning environment, that is best suited to the type of education and student selected. This atmosphere will determine the nature of the discipline to be practiced at the school.

The people behind Collegiate decided that the school was going to try to offer an exceptional classical education to above-average students, with the curriculum concentrating on (but not confined to) the basics of English, history, math, and science. If a child was well grounded in these subjects we felt he would find it much easier to master the remaining academic disciplines.

Having decided upon the curriculum, the question of atmosphere virtually took care of itself. For the students to absorb fully a classical education would require hard, concentrated study. Collegiate encourages student social activities, athletics, and other nonacademic pursuits, but when classes are in session the headmaster and teachers encourage only hard, concentrated study.

This atmosphere requires the establishment of an environment where disciplined study is an honor and sign of achievement, and it requires the disciplining of individual students who, by their actions, are disrupting the environment and infringing on the rights that other students (and parents) have acquired through payment of tuition. Discipline on these terms becomes a natural, logical outgrowth of the education the school is offering, not an arbitrary standard of conduct conceived only for purposes of exerting authority.

In the beginning I personally had mixed feelings on the question of discipline at Collegiate School. I have a philosophical aversion to authoritarian coercion and regulations, and did not want to inflict something on others that I was not willing to submit to myself. Pulling in the opposite direction was the realization that the type of education we all wanted Collegiate to offer made some degree of discipline essential. However, the fact that the school's customers would know of its standards and would be expected to have considered the matter before applying satisfied me.

Nobody was forced to attend Collegiate School. In those cases where people *are* compelled to do something, I believe a successful argument can be made that the same people should not be subjected to additional compulsion as to, for example, the length of their hair, their style of dress, or their general deportment. An institution which uses public funds indiscriminately should not be permitted to discriminate against members of the public using its services.

This is plainly not the situation in those cases where people choose to patronize a business of their own free will, and in doing so at least tacitly accept the institution's rules. In a similar situation, I assume that an applicant for employment in my business accepts the conditions of employment, or else he will quit should he find conditions obnoxious to him.

In voluntary situations the question facing the customer is: What is more important to me, the institution's product or freedom from its authority over me? If a private school requires students to wear lavender uniforms or not to smile during lunch, the customer must decide whether the education is worth acceptance of the rules. Likewise, with a school that imposes *no rules* on its students, the customer decides if this is the situation for him. The customer in a free education market finds the school offering the curriculum that meets his needs, and then determines whether the institution is acceptable in its entirety—including its rules and discipline.

Ideally, the question of what constitutes "proper" discipline and responsible behavior toward others would be settled in the student's home and the school would play no part. I feel very strongly about the parents' right to guide the lives of the children they give life to, and regret it when the school has to become involved. It is evident, however, that many parents do not exert this influence, for whatever reason. The school must then either reject the student or assume the role of disciplinarian if its standards are to be maintained.

Collegiate School has never relied on a long list of rules

and regulations for its discipline. School administrators who concoct a lengthy string of "dos and don'ts" for students are just asking for trouble. Sooner or later an exception will come along and a rule will be bent, and rules that are bendable are worse than none at all. Once a child spots a "rule" being interpreted differently for different children, the school has lost the purpose and effectiveness of its discipline.

The few rules that Collegiate does have exist primarily to let students know that there are limits to what they may do, and what these limits are in certain areas. Establishing these limits is the function of the discipline found at Collegiate. The students know how far they can go without being reprimanded for disrupting the class or school, and they appreciate the school's honesty in telling them.

Collegiate's headmaster makes the decisions concerning general school discipline and each teacher sets the classroom standards. Giving the teachers disciplinary authority could possibly lead to a wide range of highly arbitrary codes of conduct, with each classroom having a different atmosphere. This hasn't happened with us.

Collegiate's teachers know they are fully in charge of their separate "business," and part of their responsibility is keeping order. If a teacher does not maintain order, he or she will hear about it. The other teachers will complain about commotion caused by rowdy students. The parents will complain that they are not getting what they paid for. And students who want to learn will be highly intolerant of disorderly colleagues should the teacher be overly indulgent.

At the same time, Collegiate teachers realize they cannot give the boot to every student who rubs them the wrong way or speaks out of turn. When the situation gets so bad that a disruptive student must be dismissed by the headmaster, it could possibly reflect as much on the teacher as on the student. The teachers also understand that dismissals from the school mean lost income and that excessive discipline is uneconomical.

The main reason why I believe it is wise to have the individual teacher in charge of classroom discipline is that, when it is necessary, discipline must be exactly like a reward: immediate and substantial. Any time lost between the student's infraction and his punishment means that the effect is diminished. In most cases a reprimand from the teacher—and the reaction from students who are trying to learn—will be sufficient to curb a disruptive student. If this is not enough, Collegiate teachers have the authority to require a student to give up a weekend day and do work around the school—a very productive form of "discipline." Even these cases, however, are increasingly rare.

There was a period early in Collegiate's history when the enrollment took a sudden jump upward and the number of disciplinary problems increased accordingly. The teachers had been using very little discipline when the school was small and then tended to overreact to the new situation, recommending dismissal of students right and left.

The trustees put a stop to this practice by reminding the teachers, and the headmaster, that every student dismissed represented a reduction of income for the school, and this loss would eventually affect salaries. Since then Collegiate has had only isolated cases of teachers, usually new and inexperienced, who thought that harsh discipline meant the same as classroom control.

As the school has grown and matured academically, the discipline has become much more subtle. The students are aware of Collegiate's standards when they arrive, they realize that at this school hard study and academic achievement are a mark of honor, and they do a very good job at disciplining themselves. If a new youngster steps out of line, one of our "veterans" will most likely set him straight and the headmaster or teachers will probably never hear a thing about the incident.

Self-control is the best form of government and self-discipline has been the most effective disciplinary practice for Collegiate School. As the students come to appreciate this opportunity, the more responsible—and serious—they become. True freedom comes when a person has freedom to abuse and does not.

Two recent experiences at Collegiate demonstrate some of the points I have mentioned here concerning discipline. The first involved an attempt by the dean of women to lay down a rule regarding length of girls' skirts—nothing more than three inches above the knee, I believe the regulation read. The girl students didn't like it and neither did many parents. After conferences with some of the parents and talks with the students, the headmaster and the dean decided that the rule could not be realistically enforced. What looked good on one girl looked terrible on another. The school quietly dropped the rule, the girls have maintained a decorous standard of dress on their own, and there has never been another word said about this "issue."

The second situation concerned that hobgoblin of modern education—drugs. A student was using and passing around marijuana at a school function; the headmaster was told of it by some concerned students and he was about to expel the boy from school. The students objected. They argued that, since there had been no rule regarding penalties for drug-users, it was unfair to impose an arbitrary punishment on this one boy. The headmaster agreed. After this, he said, anyone using or pushing drugs in school or at school functions would be expelled. The students knew that there was now a limit in this area and there has been only one dismissal due to drug use since that time.

11

Final Thoughts

IN REALITY, I probably won't have my final thought about Collegiate School until the day I die. It has been too much a part of my physical and intellectual life to be dismissed from mind before then. But, insofar as this description of the school goes, there are a couple of final general subjects that should be touched upon. One is specific advice (including a few things I intend to do differently next time) on how others can do just what we have done at Collegiate—start their own school. The second is an attempt to describe the personal experience of my wife and me with the school, an experience that is, in every way, almost indescribable. We learn by trying.

Do It Yourself

I am convinced that it is easier to start an independent school today than it was in 1959, when Collegiate School started. Public attitudes toward education have changed a good deal since then, and parents are much more receptive toward honest exploration of alternatives to public education.

If people interested in starting such a school have any question about public attitudes in their area, they should take a market survey. I never would have proposed this when Collegiate was beginning because all I was interested in then was educating my own children, no matter what it took or what market existed.

To someone today, I would suggest they send a questionnaire to a sampling of the community, asking those who are interested in an independent school to fill in and return a form or make a telephone call. Then they would have substantial evidence of interest to show potential investors and other customers.

No matter how much public attitudes change, however, the success of an independent school still depends on the commitment of those behind the idea. I could say that a school needed an area with a population of at least 50,000 to have sufficient customers, but this might be too little or too large, depending on how hard its supporters want to work to make the school successful.

This type of venture demands substantial sacrifice, of time, money, energy, social activities, and other important items. The parents and teachers have to be aware of this and make their commitment accordingly. I do not believe a school can survive when the parents are motivated by a political consideration—such as a reaction to busing or to forced integration. Politics are ephemeral and attitudes change quickly. Commitment to a school must run deeper than politics and must concern quality educational service. Schools which thrive momentarily on a political appeal must change their ways or plan on a short, ineffectual life.

As for development of a new school, Collegiate provides an excellent working model: begin with a few grades, expanding as market demand increases and the school acquires a reputation for quality. To start off with a big operation, with hundreds of seats to fill and high overhead costs to pay, is just asking for trouble.

Another private school started in Wichita at the same time that Collegiate began. It was a church-affiliated venture, kindergarten through grade twelve. The whole operation was set in motion at once. The first year the school had debts of over $100,000 and by the end of the second year it was out of business.

Begin with a preschool, because there is a tremendous demand for it and no competition from the public schools. After this the growth of the school will depend upon the market. Find out through market surveys and conversations with parents what the demand is and what it will support in terms of school development.

There are all sorts of combinations a school can grow with. There might be enough demand to support just the preschool in the beginning. Then, after the first year, the parents may decide they want to keep their children in this sort of independent setup and will create demand for a kindergarten, first grade, etc.

On the other hand, the market may be so great that a preschool through third, or even sixth, grade is possible. The school can add one grade at a time, or wait until its reputation develops and add several grades at once.

I would advise against getting into a seventh grade and on up through high school until the people behind the school feel they know what they are doing and the lower school is financially self-sufficient. In the higher grades the costs for materials, teachers, and facilities become much greater. Unless there is such a great market demand that the school can charge full-cost tuition from the outset, it will have deficits.

The question of who should own the school deserves some thought. I have been talking about parents starting schools and making the commitment, as if only they could be considered for ownership. Although this is the way it was done at Collegiate, to my mind it is not the best arrangement. Ideally, the teachers—some or all of them—would own the entire operation. Or perhaps parents could start a school and then sell it to the teachers, as I hope will happen at Collegiate. The reason for this position is that the parents begin to lose interest as soon as their children grow up and leave the school. The teachers remain behind, as interested—academically and economically—as they ever were.

Two teachers could set up a preschool and kindergarten and go into business very easily. They should find a building where rent and utilities are low and start recruiting customers. Not every business needs to start with a new factory. In a couple of years the school will have established a reputation and will be able to project enough income that it can obtain traditional financing and build a new facility, if needed.

As the market demand increases, the original two teachers can hire others and expand the number of grades. A school offering preschool through sixth-grade classes needs eight good teachers who can run their own little businesses, and a secretary in the office to handle bookkeeping and correspondence. This is the way to keep overhead down and maintain an efficient operation.

The need for a headmaster does not arise until the school begins adding upper grades. Then you need someone to administer a growing business, plan the curriculum, counsel on college applications, and handle all the social problems that older students seem to have. But until the school reaches that point in its development, the need for a headmaster is considerably less.

If a school must have financial backers, as Collegiate did, the group should be kept small and limited to those who are willing to make a lasting commitment to the school's success. Also, the trustees should all be parents of students in the school. Another way is to sell shares to parents, who can resell the shares when their children have graduated. This is a common practice among country clubs and other associations requiring large initial capital outlays.

A school operating under full-cost pricing on a very efficient level should be financially self-sufficient within three years, at the least. After that the parents and students associated with the school will sell it to their friends and keep it going. I know it can be done.

The Personal Side

Had my wife and I foreseen all the problems we would encounter in undertaking an independent educational endeavor, we probably would not have made the effort. Having said that, let me quickly add that neither of us would hesitate to do it all over again.

If man were perceptive enough to know all the problems and difficulties that lay ahead, a majority might well give up soon after birth. But we didn't know what was in store for us, so we went ahead, trying to do our best. Only after the full course had been run could we judge whether or not the attempt had been worthwhile. Now that our three children have graduated from Collegiate, I think I can say with a reasonable amount of objectivity that our endeavor has been as rewarding an experience as two people could ever hope for.

It would be wrong to imply that we had absolutely no idea of what might happen when we took our children out of public school and, later, when we started to set up an independent school. The state-run schools and their church-run cousins were firmly entrenched in Wichita, and people who entertained any contrary ideas were usually thought of as "snobs" or "nuts," or had their youngsters labeled "problem children." We were doing something truly radical in a notoriously provincial community.

Our social apprehensions were confirmed the second we put our children in a nonpublic school. Many persons with whom we had enjoyed friendly relations up to that time were now cold, sometimes hostile. Whether they felt challenged, insulted, or otherwise offended by our action, I cannot say. It is not important to ascribe motives here, just to describe a fact.

The most unfortunate negative reaction to our educational venture came from relatives. My parents did not approve of Collegiate. They did not see why it was necessary. *Their* children had gone through the public school system and they were—bless 'em—pleased with the results. My older sister's children were beyond the school's age limits when we started, but my younger sister immediately enrolled her three youngsters in Collegiate. This was not the cozy family arrangement it might appear to be. When problems arose at the school involving my nieces and nephews, Uncle Bob was expected to smooth things out. I refused to do a thing. Such matters were to be handled entirely by the teachers and headmaster.

My wife's brother offers another case history. He was (and is) a fine and fair man, flatly opposed to the idea of independent education. Unlike the relations on my side of the family, he never once expressed any interest or acceptance of our devotion to independent education and Collegiate School. Later he was elected to the Wichita Board of Education and eventually became president of it. Remaining true to his philosophy of education, he did everything he could to improve the city's public schools. He found he could accomplish little except increase his own frustration. The bureaucrats and their red tape got the best of my brother-in-law and just like our Mr. Public Education in an earlier chapter, he chose not to stand for re-election when his first term as school board president was completed.

I have often wondered why so many people that I have observed choose to devote their time and energy exclusively to reforming public institutions when the results are so obviously frustrating and my experience has been so satisfying and rewarding. I guess that they devote their time to reforming public schools because they have come to believe that that is where the answer to their problem lies and they discount other approaches. But the reader may ask, isn't it important to reform the public schools? What if everyone followed your example? My answer is, the influence of Collegiate in presenting an alternative is the best case for public school reform that I have seen.

Collegiate was not organized to provide social activities for the parents involved. It just happened that the effort to start a new school brought together people who grew to be close friends, brought them together in ways that were new and challenging, and the close bond that resulted had as much to do with Collegiate's continuation and success as any other single factor.

A good deal of this camaraderie developed around the school's athletic events. These were strictly improvisational affairs for the first few years, and the makeshift quality served to heighten the spirit of friendship. When Collegiate added an eighth and a ninth grade, the boys started playing basketball against larger local schools on a scrimmage basis. When our players got into foul-trouble late in the game, Collegiate would sometimes end the game with only four players on the floor.

Collegiate's first football game was against a team from a town named Viola, southwest of Wichita. There was no kickoff and no punting, because we could not afford to lose any boys to injuries. Our football team played in small Kansas towns that I (a native Kansan) had never heard of, and a majority of the parents usually went along to cheer for the team. We could not afford to spend one penny on anything except academics, so when it came to sports the parents volunteered to drive, coach, lead the cheers, look after the meager equipment, and carry the water.

Whenever Collegiate hosted a game, the parents gathered before it started for some *al fresco* dining. Everyone brought a different dish, and station-wagon tailgates were converted into buffet tables. Later the auto headlights were turned on so the boys could finish the game.

Parents who don't share such experiences with their children are missing the greatest joys of life. Some businessmen get tied up in projects that keep them away from their families, but I was always looking for things to do that would bring us closer. I got enjoyment out of the smallest activities. By driving children to school I learned that a group of youngsters will soon ignore the presence of an adult and talk among themselves, and if the adult can keep his mouth shut he will learn a great deal—as I did.

Ever since becoming involved with Collegiate I have felt sorry for men who think that the education of their children is the wife's job. Not only are they failing to give their children what guidance and understanding they can offer, but they are depriving themselves of precious happiness. In the future, I'm afraid, many of them will look back and wonder what they missed, why their family life seems so empty.

If a man looks only at the facts and figures of life, he will miss the important things. The personal side cannot be measured by statistics. And to those who would ask who can judge what the "important things" are, I would say only that, for me, nothing was ever more important than spending all the time I could with the children for whom I was—with my wife—responsible.

I feel that I have had a measure of success in business, and I hope that I will be able to leave my family in a comfortable financial position. But they could lose the money in a minute. All the material gain in the world is useless without the ability to think and to reason. A man can give his children values, ideals, and an education which can never be lost, stolen, or destroyed.

You must be a zealot to be involved in independent

education, whether as parent, teacher, or headmaster. There will be opposition and discouragement, and it takes a strong commitment and a tough constitution to deal with them. And, in the end, you might fail.

Every business proposition in which I have been involved has been a gamble, and the independent-school proposition was exactly that. If a business gamble pays off, it reaffirms the reputation of the people and the product. The Collegiate gamble has paid off in the same way.

It did not fail, and the success of the school and, more important, the experience of growing and learning with our children made it immensely worthwhile. Our dearest friendships came as a result of Collegiate. Countless values and philosophical beliefs were shaped by the effort to establish a school.

Collegiate has made me a better businessman, as it taught me how to conduct business in another field, how to deal with different types of people with different areas of experience from my own. I also believe that Collegiate made me a better person.

I refuse to believe that the Collegiate venture was either miraculous or extraordinary, that it could have happened only in this place, at this time, with these people. It was a matter of wanting to control our own lives, of taking the risks that would improve our lives, and of accepting the responsibilities which the failure or the success of those risks would bring. Anyone can do this.

Index

Index